Literary Representations of Japan

At the Intersection of David Mitchell and Haruki Murakami's Worlds

Eugenia Prasol
Nagasaki University, Japan

Series in Literary Studies

VERNON PRESS

Copyright © 2024 Vernon Press, an imprint of Vernon Art and Science Inc, on behalf of the author.

All rights reserved. No part of this publication may be reproduced, stored in a retrieval system, or transmitted in any form or by any means, electronic, mechanical, photocopying, recording, or otherwise, without the prior permission of Vernon Art and Science Inc.
www.vernonpress.com

In the Americas:
Vernon Press
1000 N West Street, Suite 1200,
Wilmington, Delaware 19801
United States

In the rest of the world:
Vernon Press
C/Sancti Espiritu 17,
Malaga, 29006
Spain

Series in Literary Studies

Library of Congress Control Number: 2023936071

ISBN: 978-1-64889-911-9

Also available: 978-1-64889-674-3 [Hardback]; 978-1-64889-749-8 [PDF, E-Book]

Product and company names mentioned in this work are the trademarks of their respective owners. While every care has been taken in preparing this work, neither the authors nor Vernon Art and Science Inc. may be held responsible for any loss or damage caused or alleged to be caused directly or indirectly by the information contained in it.

Every effort has been made to trace all copyright holders, but if any have been inadvertently overlooked the publisher will be pleased to include any necessary credits in any subsequent reprint or edition.

Cover design by Vernon Press. Cover image by JL G from Pixabay.

Acknowledgements

I would like to express my deepest appreciation to my academic supervisor Professor Suzuki Akiyoshi without whose careful guidance and unwavering support this work would have been impossible; to my first supervisor and mentor, Professor Lipina Victoria, who always encouraged me in my academic pursuits; and to my mum who has always believed in me.

Table of Contents

Acknowledgements — iii

Foreword — vii

Introduction — ix

Chapter 1
Murakami Haruki's Works as Intertextual Component of the Representation of Japan in the "Japanese" Novels of David Mitchell — 1

1.1 Problem Statement — 1

1.2 Murakami Haruki: A Brief Outline of the Intercultural Influences on His Work — 3

1.3 David Mitchell: The Writing Path and Creative Orienteers — 4

1.4 Intertextuality, Literary Influences and the Image of Japan in the Works of Murakami Haruki and David Mitchell — 8

1.5 Conclusion — 21

Chapter 2
The Concept of Techno-Orientalism and Techno-Images of Japan in the Works of Murakami Haruki and David Mitchell — 23

2.1 Perceptions of Japan through Different Types of Orientalism — 23

    2.1.1 Orientalism — 23

    2.1.2 Self-Orientalism — 25

    2.1.3 Techno-Orientalism — 26

2.2 Techno-Images of Japan in the Works of David Mitchell and Murakami Haruki — 28

    2.2.1 "Japanese" Novels by David Mitchell through the Concepts of Techno-Orientalism and Remediation — 29

    2.2.2 Dystopian Features of Techno-Images in Murakami's Works — 37

2.3 Conclusion — 42

Chapter 3
Representations of Violence as Part of the Image of Japan in the Works of David Mitchell and Murakami Haruki 43
3.1 Theoretical Background and Types of Violence 43
3.2 Murakami's Position on Violence 46
3.3 Intertextuality of the Religious Violence in David Mitchell's *Ghostwritten* 50
3.4 Comparative Analysis of the Representations of Religious Violence 53
3.5 Individual and Domestic Violence in Murakami's Works 60
3.6 Historical Violence in Murakami's Representations of Wartime Japan 61
3.7 Aesthetisation and Deconstruction of the Samurai Ethics in *Number9Dream* 72
3.8 Conclusion 76

Conclusion 77

References 83

Index 89

Foreword

Many authors, not only in Japan but throughout the world, write about Japan, including James Clavell (e.g., *Shogun*, 1975), David Mitchell (e.g., *Thousand Autumns on Dejima*, 2010), William Gibson (e.g., *Neuromancer*, 1984; *Pattern Recognition*, 2003), *Ming Jin Lee* (e.g., *Pachinko*, 2017), and others. In their works, some writers use common global stereotypes or re-creations of stereotypes, for example, aesthetic Japan, traditional and exotic Japan, military Japan, imperialistic Japan, Techno-Orientalist Japan, globalized Japan, Japan as an economic miracle, and Japan as a yellow peril. Other writers, however, go beyond the stereotypes to create new images of Japan.

Interestingly, unlike previous writers, the Japanese author Haruki Murakami depicts Japan with little use of stereotypes, while the British author David Mitchell, who was greatly influenced by Murakami and who declared he would go beyond Murakami's literary description, depicts Japan in Orientalist-like ways. This strange master-disciple relationship has long been a mystery; however, its elucidation will shed new light on writers' representations of Japan and on Murakami and Mitchell's works.

Eugenia Prasol's *Literary Representations of Japan: At the Intersection of David Mitchell and Haruki Murakami's Worlds* attempts to unravel that mystery through a comparative analysis of Murakami and Mitchell's literary texts to present a theory of representation of "Japan". According to Prasol, Mitchell's heavy use of exotic imagery is not because he is an Orientalist, but rather because he portrays Japan as seen from a Western perspective. Both Murakami and Mitchell's representations depart from traditional stereotypes, but the difference between them lies in Japan as seen by the Japanese and as seen by contemporary Westerners. They are both correct images; together, they represent Japan's global image. In this sense, Murakami and Mitchell's texts complementarily describe Japan through an East-West cultural dialogue.

Thus, Prasol's work presents a new theory of Japanese representation and literature by viewing Murakami and Mitchell's intertextuality as a representation by an insider and an outsider—as described by Edward Said. By a persuasive argument with abundant citations to Murakami and Mitchell's texts and previous studies, as well as to previous studies on images, Orientalism, violence, and so on, Prasol's *Literary Representations of Japan* contributes significantly to studies on Japan's representation and on Murakami and Mitchell's works.

Prasol became a full lecturer at Oles Honchar Dnipro National University in Ukraine after she graduated from its master's program. She had researched Japanese literary texts, for instance, those of Soseki Natume, Ogai Mori, and Haruki Murakami, and published good academic articles. More than a decade ago, she generated the idea for the research project in *Literary Representations of Japan*. Having earned a master's degree, she asked me whether she could enter the doctoral program at our university in Japan, where I could supervise her dissertation. I readily agreed, but I did not hear from her again until two years later, when she told me that the Japanese Ministry of Education, Culture, Sports, Science and Technology had selected her as a Japanese government-sponsored foreign student. By that time, I had moved to another university with a humanities graduate school still in the planning stages. Moreover, we did not know whether a master's and a doctoral program simultaneously or only a master's program could first be established. Nevertheless, Prasol came to Japan and continued her studies as a research student. When it became clear that a master's program had to be created first, I wanted to write a recommendation letter to introduce her to another graduate school. However, she remained at our university, saying that she would continue our master's program. Her master's thesis was evaluated as outstanding, of course, and this book is based on it. I believe the book's workmanship is at the level of a doctoral dissertation, and it surely opens a significant new perspective on studies of Japan's representation and of Murakami and Mitchell, illuminating their works as an East-West cultural dialogue.

Akiyoshi Suzuki
Professor of American and Comparative Literature and East-West Studies
Nagasaki University, Japan

Introduction[1]

In recent decades in the world of humanities, the issues of national perception have come to the fore. This is due to the peculiarities of the development of the academic knowledge itself: without clarification of the laws of the national perception, it is impossible to understand the intercultural dialogue as a whole. In a rather simplified way, we may assume that the world culture is determined by a combination of opposite processes of divergence (national identification and unification) and convergence of cultures (globalization and Westernization). Japanese culture is no exception and can be considered in these terms just as well. It is well-known that the modern Japanese context, marked by the phenomenon of cross-cultural interaction, provides numerous examples of reconstructing the image of Japan in literary texts as well as rethinking the poetics and semantics of postmodernist models of the West in unity with the national tradition and authentic artistic and aesthetic canon.

The image of a certain country is, at first glance, an unambiguous term, which hides in itself the plurality of distinct, and sometimes opposing in their content and ways of formation phenomena: symbols, stereotypes, clichés, biases, etc. The image of Japan in the works of contemporary Western and Japanese authors is often an implicit, metaphysical concept with a large number of meanings, which are always shifting and unstable due to the variety of historical, political, economic, cultural and literary factors. A bias in the perception of oriental cultures is evident in the works of many researchers as well as in the works of many writers, who have repeatedly emphasised the impossibility of understanding between East and West.

The portrayal of Japan in Western culture and literature has its own history. Particularly controversial and complex are the Japanese phenomena in the twentieth and twenty-first centuries. The exotic image of a beautiful country of cherry blossoms, resilient samurais and picturesque geisha is replaced by the propaganda cartoons of the "yellow peril", which in their turn give room to the technological and anti-utopian visions of Japan, the country of the future. Another complexity in branching and systematizing the images of Japan is related to the contrasting vision from inside and outside. "Objectivity" of the image from the outside is often accused of the Orientalist approach, which pays special attention to the exotic functions of Japaneseness and aesthetics in the culture of this country.

---

[1] This research is based on my Master thesis

Similar to those of other Asian countries, the images of Japan are constructed on the basis of two main approaches: it is either an underlined vision of Japan's femininity in its elegance or the notions of its aggressive and violent character. However, Japanese culture occupies a special place in the context of contemporary Western culture due to the unique combination of Eastern sensitivity and the achievements of technical progress. Representations of modernized Japan are augmented with high technologies, creating an image of a country focused on the idea of financial and economic success. It is needless to say that such views may well be quite divorced from reality. Such stereotypes fall under the definition of techno-orientalism, which is well-known in literature because of the genre of cyberpunk. This genre is marked by the distinct perspective on Japan as a soulless superpower which is to be hated and afraid of. The best examples can be found in the works of famous representatives of the genre, such as William Gibson, Bruce Sterling and Philip K. Dick, who influenced to some extent the works of Murakami Haruki and David Mitchell, shaping their own perceptions of the techno-images of Japan. The concern is with the assessment of the state of the Japanese culture, the tendencies of development and the destruction of spirituality. Thus, the attention of Western writers is focused on the futuristic arrangement of the Japanese theme. It is no coincidence that the images of Japan in both Japanese and Western literature always exist in the field of the influence of one of the opposite stereotypes – 1) Japan's traditional aesthetics and culture; and 2) Japan, which loses its past, becomes modernized and robotic.

In the context of such an ideologised discourse of orientalism in general and techno-orientalism in particular, the relevance of studying the images of Japanese uniqueness becomes acute. At a time when the West builds its own image of rationality and superiority through its relations with Japan, Japan itself also defines its position, emphasising its geographical and cultural uniqueness. Important components of these representations are the victim mentality and the idea of the incomprehensibility of the Japanese soul. Those aspects are at the centre of artistic comprehension and interpretation of contemporary writers who try to look into Japan from the inside (Kawabata Yasunari, Tanizaki Junichiro, Oe Kenzaburo, Shimada Masahiko, Murakami Ryu, etc.) and outside (William Gibson, Roger Zelazny, James G. Ballard, Kazuo Ishiguro). Murakami and Mitchell are among them. However, those stereotypes are not permanent as well; they also change over time according to historical circumstances. When relations between Western countries and Japan are good, as in the early twentieth century or in the 1960s, the aesthetic visions of Japan in the West tend to predominate. First, it was Pierre Loti with his *Madame Chrysanthème* (1887) and then Puccini's *Madam Butterfly* (1904) that were considered the key texts in moulding Western attitudes toward Japan at the turn of the twentieth century. In the post-war period, it was Ruth Benedict's *The Chrysanthemum and the Sword* (1946) which depicted Japan in a highly aesthetic way. Kawabata Yasunari, the Noble Prize laureate in literature in 1968, can also be considered a writer who, to some extent, meets the specific Western expectations in regard to Japan with its unique sense of beauty and expression. The proof of that can be found in the Noble Prize given to Kawabata Yasunari in 1968, whose aesthetic view of Japan was admired by the West.

An interesting tendency in the representation of Japan should be noted. When relations were worsened, either during the war or after the tensions in the trade relations of the 1980s, the "warrior of Japan" became dominant in the representation of the country. The most distinctive literary examples of that can be found in Michael Crichton's controversial novel *The Rising Sun* (1992) and in the sci-fi genre of cyberpunk mentioned above. Although the power of stereotypes remains unquestionable, these fluctuations leave space for alternative images, which may as well be independent of clichés and mainstream biases. In this research, I examine Japaneseness in the works of Murakami Haruki and David Mitchell as the essence of Japanese national identity, the peculiarity of their world perception and their way of thinking.

At the end of the twentieth century and the beginning of the twenty-first century, the formation of an updated image of Japan started in the works of English and Japanese authors. Studying the image of Japan, which is now part of cultural, political, historical and literary discourses, requires an interdisciplinary approach involving studies of Japanese history, culture, philosophy, and aesthetics. In modern conditions, to write truthfully about something as complicated as Japan often means avoiding generalizations and ideological or aesthetic considerations. According to numerous researchers (among them are the prominent works of Roland Barthes (1983), Jacques Derrida (1985, 1997), Koichi Iwabuchi (1994, 2002), Kojin Karatani (1989, 1993, 1999, 2011), John Lie (2004), Ian Littlewood (2007), Masao Miyoshi (1991), Takayuki Tatsumi (2006), Karen Thornber (2009), etc.), Japan remains a country of unshakable stereotypes, and even the Japanese themselves contribute to such a state of things often adding up to the existing stereotypes about Japan. In this research, the categorisation of such generalizations will be checked by the analysis of specific cultural and literary material. The purpose of this book, therefore, is to determine the basis for representing the image of Japan in the novels of the Japanese writer Murakami Haruki and the English writer David Mitchell, to discover the similarities and differences in the representation of Japan in theme, problematic and intertextual levels.

My research focuses on a comparative analysis of the Japanese and English prose written in the last decades and examines constant, stereotypical and historically changing features of the literary image of Japan in the writings of David Mitchell and Murakami Haruki, as well as the discursive ways that are used by scholars such as Roland Barthes (1983), Kojin Karatani (1989, 1993, 1999, 2012), Edward Said (1979, 1993), etc. It helps to see the ways in which imagery and concepts are activated in the discourse on Japaneseness. The primary reference is not to the empirical reality of Japan but to intertextuality in English and Japanese prose. Bringing forth new imagological problems of contemporary comparative studies and broadly historical, sociological, cultural and literary contexts allows the unveiling of the paradigm of representing Japan, at the core of which is auto-image – a theory of Japaneseness (*nihonjinron*). The emphasis of this research is on a range of stereotypes and their artistic deconstruction by Murakami Haruki and David Mitchell. The in-depth comparative analysis gives grounds to reveal the interrelated aspects in the image of Japan. Traditional stereotyping of Japan as exotic, mysterious, strange, irrational, sensual and potentially dangerous is juxtaposed with literary images of the country in the works of Murakami and Mitchell that reveal the variety of complex paradigmatic components of the image of Japan (exotic, violent, odourless, techno-orientalist, etc.). This study evokes the enduring themes in national identity debates that are substantially reworked in contemporary theories of Japaneseness (Ruth Benedict (1967), Peter Dale (1986), Naoki Sakai (1998), Harumi Befu (1987), Sugimoto Yoshio (1986), etc.) thereby determining the reasons for the longevity of stereotypes and understanding the complex phenomenon of shifting formulations of "Japan" as an aestheticized object. This research expands the knowledge of Japan as a set of meanings, tracing not only the common features but also delving into their historical evolution, multidimensional nature, specific artistic deconstruction and recontextualization. The ultimate goal of this research is to advance the understanding of how both general and specific components of literary representations of Japan and Japaneseness are manifested in the East-West cultural dialogue.

The research material for this book is, as mentioned earlier, the works of Murakami Haruki and the "Japanese" novels of David Mitchell. The choice of these two authors is not coincidental. Murakami has had a great influence on Mitchell's writing, and Mitchell himself admitted on numerous occasions that he tried his best to learn from Murakami in his pursuit of a writing path. That most certainly creates a strong link between the two authors, which is only deepened by all the intertextual relationships between their novels. As I will try to prove later, Mitchell intertextually implements a lot of Murakami's topics and techniques, creating a certain intercultural dialogue in representing Japan. Nevertheless, it would be impossible to claim that Murakami is the only intertextual source for Mitchell's novels – by all means, there are other Western and Japanese writers that Mitchell refers. However, being contemporary authors, both of them share the modern social and cultural context, which is why it is important to study their literary relationship closely while researching the renovated image of Japan and the postmodern deconstruction of the stereotypes related to Japan and Japaneseness. Keeping in mind the link between the two authors and their new view on old concepts, I research the semantic and poetic peculiarities of a postmodern reconstruction of the orientalist image of Japanese uniqueness in polemics with the tradition existing in the West and East.

It is noteworthy that both Murakami and Mitchell are quite conscious of creating and renewing the image of Japan while undermining and deconstructing the existing and widely spread stereotypes. Thus, Murakami addresses this problem directly, devoting his non-fiction work *Underground* (1997-1998), among others, to the investigation of what modern Japan has become and how it is possible to consider some darker sides of Japan, such as terrorism, to be still part of Japan. Mitchell follows in the footsteps of his older colleague, trying "to do what Haruki Murakami does, depicting Japan as it is, and finding the beauty in the ugliness" (Mitchell 2014, para. 17), bringing up everything that there is to Japan, no matter how ugly it can be, and raising it to a new level.

This research consists of three main parts. In the first chapter, "Murakami Haruki's Works as Intertextual Component of the Representation of Japan in 'Japanese' Novels of David Mitchell", I aim to present the two writers as well as analyse all the affinities and common features in their works and to present in what ways Mitchell references Murakami and intertextually invites the Japanese author into his text. The focus of this chapter is on the image of Japan as a country which is unique in its immutable tradition, as well as its radical revision in Murakami's and Mitchell's fiction in the aspect of modern ideas about Japan based on the ideas developed by Roland Barthes (1983), Iwabuchi Koichi (1994, 2002), Karatani Kojin (1989, 1993, 1999, 2012), Miyoshi Masao (1991), etc. Here I argue that the general denominator of Mitchell's artistic concepts is Murakami's novels. As Mitchell pointed out himself, "I had a crush on Murakami" (Mitchell 2009, para. 7). The English writer considers his purpose to revise the Orientalist point of view on Japan: "I wanted to do what Haruki Murakami does, depicting Japan as it is, and finding the beauty in the ugliness" (Mitchell 2014, para. 17). Some researchers, such as Philip Childs (2011) and Bairon Tenson Posadas (2011) who considerably simplify this phenomenon of creative consonance, call Mitchell the "intertextual doppelganger" (Posadas 2011, p. 97) of Murakami, counting the quotations and references, while leaving out the main point in Mitchell's "Japanese" novels – creative polemics with the Japanese writer, intertextual gaining of new meanings in regards to the image of Japan. The intertextuality of Mitchell's novels is not limited to just quoting but rather appears to be an attempt (and quite a successful one at that) to participate in East-West dialogue in regard to the image of Japan.

The second chapter, "Techno-Orientalism and Techno-Images of Japan in the Works of David Mitchell and Murakami Haruki", is divided into a few parts of its own. In "Perceptions of Japan through Different Types of Orientalism", I offer a brief overlook of the theoretical framework, which I use for further analysis in this chapter. I address the ongoing debate on Orientalism and look closely into the evolution of Orientalist conceptions in regard to representing Japan. The chapter focuses on a variety of exotic images that have undergone significant transformations over the centuries and yet remain fundamentally orientalist. In "Techno-Images of Japan in the Works of David Mitchell and Murakami Haruki", the image of modern Japan is considered not only as the deconstruction of stereotypical representations of Western cultural discourse, but also as a reconstruction and remediation of techno culture such as cyberspace, computer games and so on. I try to trace the techno-images that Mitchell and Murakami use in their novels, formulating and recreating the image of Japan. Such an image of the country is formed because of the existing stereotypes, but it also goes against them, reformulating, complementing and correcting newly emerging ideological prejudices. My purpose here is to search how the authors address the futuristic image of Japan, how it is related to the notions of Orientalism and by what means the writers defy possible stereotypical meanings of it.

In the third chapter, "Representations of Violence as Part of the Image of Japan in the Works of David Mitchell and Murakami Haruki", the focus is on another famous image/stereotype of Japan as a country of violence in the eyes of the West, is often associated with, but not limited to, the ethics of samurai. This image is widely manifested and deeply deconstructed in Murakami Haruki's and David Mitchell's work. As I demonstrate, the authors address this issue differently, using their own particular set of images, characters and situations. This only proves that Mitchell does not duplicate the novels written by Murakami but rather involves himself with the dialogue-polemics, which creates not just the chronicles of the modern life of Japan but the image of the unimaginable cruelty of the world in general. Despite all the differences in style and in addressing the topic of cruelty, the two authors yet somehow reach the same result creating a complex, multi-layered and somewhat controversial image of the country and people of Japan.

Based on the analysis undertaken in the abovementioned chapters of this research, it becomes clear that although there are a lot of distinctive similarities in representing Japan between Haruki Murakami and David Mitchell, there are still a few differences in their style and emphasis. The Japanese writer Murakami creates and recreates Japan without implementing any orientalist features or exotic imagery. The writer has long been known as one who attempts to depict Japan as close to its real contemporary condition as it is at all possible. On the

Introduction   xv

other hand, the English writer David Mitchell whose writing about Japan is hugely impacted by Murakami's work, nevertheless does not avoid using imagery that can be considered fairly orientalist in its essence. Here I intend to look into such phenomena closely and try to prove that his exotic images are not orientalist in its meaning but rather a parody – an ironic way of depicting Japan as it might be expected from the traditional Western perspective. I certainly cannot go as far as to call the two writers "realistic" since both create their worlds in the postmodern tradition with significant elements of magical realism, which is fairly estranged from literary realism. However, as the following research demonstrates, it is perhaps still possible to claim that both Murakami and Mitchell create Japan in the most mimetic way achievable within the bounds of contemporary literary reality, approaching "the real Japan", whatever that may mean for each of them.

Chapter 1

Murakami Haruki's Works as Intertextual Component of the Representation of Japan in the "Japanese" Novels of David Mitchell

1.1 Problem Statement

Here I research the image of Japan as a complex combination of notions and ideas comprised of national stereotypes, as well as how these stereotypes are deconstructed in the novels of Murakami Haruki and David Mitchell concerning the aspect of contemporary visions of Japan. One of the main themes of Japanese literature in the twentieth and twenty-first centuries has become the search for possible understandings of what it means to be Japanese. The most representative example of this phenomenon and its evolution can be found in the Nobel prize lectures of two Japanese writers – Kawabata Yasunari ("Japan, the Beautiful, and Myself", 1964) and Oe Kenzaburo ("Japan, the Ambiguous, and Myself", 1991), both of whom referred to themselves in connection to Japan, though defining Japan and Japaneseness in different terms. The question of understanding Japaneseness gets really complicated because of the controversial history of Japan in the twentieth century with the ups and downs of militarism and the decline of traditional Japanese culture. One of the most famous modern writers of Japan, Murakami Haruki, is not forgotten in contemplating these questions. As we attempt to prove later, it is clear from his works that Murakami looks for Japaneseness, which was also noted by researchers such as Jay Rubin, Rebecca Sutter and Susan Napier. However, it is not only Japanese writers but Western writers as well who try to understand what Japaneseness is. And one of them is English writer David Mitchell.

Yomota Inuhiko (2019) states that the works of Murakami embody transcultural ideas of the existence of modern man in the open world of today. This has become a sort of artistic guideline to Murakami's younger English colleague David Mitchell, who joins Murakami in a creative dialogue. The importance and justification of comparing the works of two writers in terms of representation of the image of Japan in English and Japanese prose are due to 1) the impact Murakami had on Mitchell (as Mitchell admitted himself); 2) the appeal of both authors to artistic representations of the modern image of Japan; 3) the relevance of the study of the East-West discourse of the modern image Japan in poststructuralist theory (Roland Barthes, 1983; Jacques Derrida, 1985). However, if Mitchell may create a hetero-image of Japan under the influence of Western discourse on Japan, the novels of Murakami are primarily an auto image of Japan, represented in the complex refraction. In order to be able to analyse the works of the two authors in this regard, however, we should look first into their respective writing paths and see how they have established and manifested themselves as writers.

Researchers estimate Murakami's work quite controversial, for there is no unity of thought and opinion regarding his work. In the works of Mitchell, on the other hand, critics see the style and tone reminiscent of the manner of Murakami. However, I am not only interested exclusively in the degree of influence of the Japanese writer on Mitchell but also in how he creates in his novels the dialogue with Murakami regarding the main object of my research – the image of Japan.

Any image, and especially the image of Japan, is, according to poststructuralist theorists, always a representation, and as a result of transnational traffic of image culture, it is always unrepresentable because it has the ability to exist only as a total sum of perceptions of it. As Posadas claims, "Japan is a signifier that is overcoded with and overdetermined by shifting constellation of relations through which it is imagined" (Posadas 2011, p. 77). Therefore, the study of how writers of East and West (in this case, Murakami and Mitchell) see this phenomenon helps to overcome the Eurocentric temptation in the understanding of the subject.

Speaking of Mitchell's prose and his constant appeals to the Japanese author and his work, it may be appropriate to recall the lines from the novel *Metroland* (2011) by Julian Barnes, another prominent English writer; the lines, which, it seems, describe perfectly well the literary relations between the two writers: "it was not a question of imitation or parody; it was more a question of trading on resonances, that most twentieth-century of techniques" (Barnes 2011, p. 126).

The importance of this comparative study of "trading on resonances" lies in the fact the English and the Japanese writers join the literary and cultural discussion on stereotypes about Japan and Japaneseness. It is clear that their appeals to the theme of Japan and Japaneseness correlate with constant views on the subject in the literary tradition and in everyday consciousness. Analysis of these points of collision could explain not only differences but also why the writers resort to revision and rethinking of established national cultural clichés and ethnotypes.

1.2 Murakami Haruki: A Brief Outline of the Intercultural Influences on His Work

Japanese writer Murakami Haruki hardly needs any introduction. As Rebecca Suter states, "Murakami is probably the most translated among contemporary Japanese writers" (Suter 2008, p. 1), which places him among the most popular writers of modern Japan. Murakami's cultural role, however, is deeper than that – while popularizing Japan in the world, he is also the one who introduces the West to Japan. Suter writes that "he has been very active in introducing American literature to Japan, having translated writers such as F. Scott Fitzgerald, John Irving, Grace Paley, Tim O'Brien, J. D. Salinger and Raymond Carver" (Suter 2008, p. 1). Among Japanese researchers who studied his work, there are Akari Chiaki, Wakaba Ogoda, Hayakawa Seishi, Kawai Hayao, etc. For the purposes of this research, I am more interested in the main features of his style and the main topics he explores. Looking closely into these phenomena will allow me to analyse his connection and intertextual dialogue with David Mitchell.

Some Japanese thinkers, including Murakami himself (Murakami and Kawai 2017, Karatani 2011), analyse Murakami's works through the lens of changes that occurred to his style and topics. Murakami's style has changed considerably from his early days to the present. The major changes, as was pointed out, were triggered by his long-term life overseas, as well as the historical events in Japan, the Great Hanshin earthquake (1995) and the Tokyo subway sarin gas attacks (1995). One of the approaches is to see the shift as the opposition of detachment versus commitment. As Murakami puts it himself, "Previously, detachment was important to me. Recently, I think a lot about commitment. Commitment has become extremely important to me, especially when I write novels"[1] (Kawai 1995, p. 18). Commitment here means having a relationship with society and individuals, and the extent of this attitude is significant if we compare his early works and his works from the late 90s onwards.

Murakami Haruki has long entered the world of literature and has a reputation as a modern classic, who has even been expected by many to win a Nobel prize in literature (which he has not done so far). As it was repeatedly stated, the author is considered the least Japanese of all existing Japanese authors. Not only is he the largest experimenter of modern Japanese literature,

---

[1] Translation is mine
以前はデタッチメント（関わりのなさ）というのがぼくにとっては大事なことだった。コミットメント（関わり）ということについて最近よく考える。小説を書くときでも、コミットメントということがぼくにとってはものすごく大事になってきた　（河合 1995, p. 18）。

but he also is popular among Western readers. Thus, the researchers call him "increasingly international and increasingly fantastic" (Napier 2005, p. 204). He works under the influence of Western, especially American, literary tradition, embodying in his work transcultural ideas of the existence of a modern man in a modern world. Some critics conclude that Murakami is one of the first Japanese writers to make an attempt to look at Japan in his works through Western eyes. For instance, Suter, in her research, defines Murakami's works as "Japanese-American cultural cross-representation" and refers to the author as "a literary and cultural mediator between Japan and the United States" (Suter 2008, p. 1). In terms of cultural knowledge, Murakami's works are mediators of intercultural dialogue texts of world culture and sources of diverse cultural information. If we look at the architecture of his novels, we can say that Murakami's works present a world of a parable, designed with recognizable symbols; but the meaning of these symbols remains uncertain. His books are full of philosophical digressions and literary allusions (almost always Western). Also, it is worth noting the writer's contribution to the world (and especially Western) pop culture. Combining, thus, in his writings Western (particularly what his characters read and what music they listen to) and Japanese elements (images of the modern post-industrial city, the problematisation of Japanese history, etc.), the author creates a specific image of the world as a small village, which, however, remains uncertain as to its identity (we will see the examples of this later when we analyse his work closely). Thus, in Murakami's works, the image of Japan emerges not as an exotic, alluring mystery, but as habitual human existence, with all its everyday problems.

1.3 David Mitchell: The Writing Path and Creative Orienteers

David Mitchell is a British writer who was trained in English and American literature and lived in Japan for 7 years. He can speak Japanese fluently, and, with help from his Japanese wife, he translated into English a book written by a 13-year-old Japanese boy Higashida Naoki *The Reason I Jump: One Boy's Voice from the Silence of Autism*. From the first of his novels (*Ghostwritten*, 1999), Mitchell has become extremely popular. The writer has attracted the attention of researchers because of his unique style and the variety of topics he explores. Currently, his work is represented by the following novels: *Ghostwritten* (1999), *Number9Dream* (2001), *Cloud Atlas* (2004), *Black Swan Green* (2006), *The Thousand Autumns of Jacob de Zoet* (2010), *The Bone Clocks* (2014), and *Slade House* (2015).

The works of the writer do not fit into clear genre boundaries: there, the signs of a variety of genres can be found – from the usual historical fiction and dark dystopian themes to literary farce. In literary criticism, the bar on the assessment of the works of Mitchell was highly raised – his style and techniques have been compared to those of Vladimir Nabokov and Umberto Eco, and the postmodern complexity of Mitchel's work has been repeatedly emphasised. Three of his novels – so far – thematise Japan: *Ghostwritten, Number9Dream,* and *The Thousand Autumns of Jacob de Zoet.*

Mitchell has been characterised as a cosmopolitan writer. Berthold Schoene, in his *The Cosmopolitan Novel* (2009), in the chapter "The World Begins Its Turn with You, or How David Mitchell's Novels Think", claims that

> Mitchell's ambition is to imagine globality by depicting worldwide human living in multifaceted, delicately entwined, serialised snapshots of the human condition, marked by global connectivity and virtual proximity as much as psychogeographical detachment and xenophobic segregation. … Mitchell's fiction summons humanity's world-creative potential as well as its tragic (self-) destructiveness into a kind of literary communality which his readers are not only invited to relate to, but must partake of as inhabitants of one and the same world (Schoene 2009, p. 98).

Although not all researchers agree that "one and the same world" results from the "world-creative potential" that Mitchell "awakens" in his readers (Patrick O'Donnell, for instance, is of the opinion that it is "rather multiple worlds traversed by mobile identities" (O'Donnell 2015, p. 5)), Schoene makes a solid point about the connectivity of Mitchell's works, which occur "across time, space, region, and domain" (Schoene 2009, p. 98).

There is a general sense that Mitchell's literary concepts are connected to the works of Murakami. As Mitchell himself noted, "I had a crush on Murakami" (Mitchell 2009, para. 7). In writing, especially in his "Japanese" books, Mitchell sees his goal in reviewing the orientalist visions of Japan: "I wanted to do what Haruki Murakami does, depicting Japan as it is, and finding the beauty in the ugliness" (Mitchell 2009, para. 17). Researcher Bairon Tenson Posadas was the first to call Mitchell the "intertextual doppelganger" (Posadas 2011, p. 97) of Murakami (starting by this a certain tradition of looking into the connection between the two authors), significantly simplifying the phenomenon of creative consonance, which can be found in the works of Murakami and Mitchell. We can even trace the tendency of just accounting the quotes, allusions, plot lines and topics, which can be thought of as common in Mitchell's and Murakami's works, and leaving without any attention to the most important – the artistic polemic of the English author with the Japanese writer and intertextual up-building of new meanings in representations of Japan.

Mitchell, who spent some years in Japan, implements his experience in his works and tries to go beyond the stereotypical Orientalist notions about this country and its culture. In an interview, the writer directly declares his tasks: "I wanted the book to travel East to West because it reverses the usual direction of Orientalism and challenges the Eurocentric view of the world map" (Mitchell

2009 para. 16). His aim as an artist immersed in the study of the image of Japan. He aspired to revise the Orientalist view of Japan, the very view formed once in the West: "I have a problem with the way Japan is usually portrayed in the West, as the land of cherry blossoms, geishas, Mt. Fuji, and kamikaze pilots. I wanted to do what Haruki Murakami does, depicting Japan as it is and finding the beauty in the ugliness" (Mitchell 2009, para. 17).

The intertextuality of Mitchell's novels cannot be reduced only to quotations; it is more a dominant part of the East-West dialogue regarding the image of Japan. Mitchell polemicizes with Murakami's principles not to refer to the stereotypical images while constructing the literary representation of Japan and ironically uses these stereotypes as well as puts more attention into such a significant problem of modern Japan as a loss of family ties, depicting the problem in the way of mimicking the plot lines of Murakami's novels. That is why the image of Japan represented in such a system of intertextual poetics loses its unambiguity. Japan, in Mitchell's works, is shown as an ultramodern world of hi-tech, as a cosy place of jazz lovers, as a cruel shadowy world of yakuza, as an asylum, and as a country of social injustice and racial bias. Creating the Japanese national and cultural image as a hetero-image – through the point of view of another nation – and then as an auto-image through the point of view of his Japanese character, Mitchell, with such a difficult system of literary techniques underlines conventionalism of dividing the perspective into Self / Other. This is not only the image of Japan as a Western picture of *japaneserie* (rare sorts of tea, colourful depiction of the cherry bloom, yakuza, etc.), but also widespread stereotypes about modern Japanese people (lifelong employment in Japanese companies, "office samurais/robots", religious sects and acts of terrorism, Americanized youth). Intertextual reading of Mitchell's novels via Murakami detects the openness of the works of an English writer who knows Japan so well.

The significant feature of the poetics of Mitchell's novels *Ghostwritten* (a few chapters) and *Number9Dream* is that the narrator/main character is always Japanese. Such a technique of speaking from the viewpoint of the Other has its long tradition (*Persian Letters* by Charles Montesquieu, 1721; *The Citizen of the World Or Letters from a Chinese Philosopher* by Oliver Goldsmith, 1760 – 61, etc.). Mentioned writers place their characters into a subordinate position and deprive them of their own subjectivity. Mitchell's "Japanese" narrative simultaneously gives ground for such an interpretation and refutes it. Mitchell constantly underlines the importance of subjective positions, about which, he says, he learned from Murakami. And in such a way, the literary violence against the Other is to be overcome, which is impossible to understand in the light of the sustainable dichotomous contrast between East and West. This extended imagological diverse specification of the image of Japan (from Fuji to everyday life in Japan) defines the modern image of the country, opposing the stereotypical image of the distant exotic East, whose representation as a cultural universality prevailed in Western literature at the end of the nineteenth and at the beginning of the twentieth century.

On some level, in his works, Mitchell simulates Japanese literature, which explores the ways of Western discourse on Orientalism and its cultural position in Japan. Most stereotypes of Orientalism / Occidentalism become simulacra (in terms of Jean Baudrillard 1994) of the game culture in a huge transcultural field. One can notice that among the many allusions in the novel primary attention is given to the direct and indirect references to the works of Murakami Haruki. Mitchell stresses that he learned an important lesson from the famous Japanese writer's works, underlining that "Murakami's novels show how literature can marry popular culture to cook up humour and metaphor" (Mitchell 2003, para. 6). However, Mitchell, as if anticipating critics' reproaches expresses his hope that "there's enough of me in the book to ensure that it's more than just a homage or an imitation of Murakami" (Mitchell 2010, para. 24).

Such possible intertextual relations of Mitchell's works with the works of Murakami bring into focus the feature of Murakami's works that researchers call "un-Japaneseness". Mitchell's text, written in English, unexpectedly defends the Japaneseness of Murakami's novels. This is due to the way of representation of Japan, which Mitchell builds through a complex system of similarities and differences in Murakami's works. Mitchell argues with his senior colleague in the process of depicting Japaneseness – for example, Mitchell intentionally uses exotic images, and Murakami does not. Furthermore, he develops (more carefully than Murakami) important topics concerning Japan, with its patriarchal traditions, the problem of the destruction of family ties, and sometimes parodying storylines of Murakami novels. Thus the image of Japan and Japaneseness represented in the system of such intertextual poetics loses uniqueness, and Japan appears as an ultramodern world of technological nightmare, as a secluded corner of a jazz-lover, as a hospital in the mountains for the mentally ill, as brutal yakuza shadow world, as a country of social inequality and racial prejudice.

Not only has this literary relationship brought together two writers, but their place in the world: the researchers call Murakami's and Mitchell's novels global and planetary. Mitchell responds to the artistic innovations of Murakami in creating the image of Japan based not only on words but also on allowing into literature images of other channels of information. Nevertheless, the main intext of Mitchel remains in Murakami's works and their reconsidering regarding the image of Japan. Mitchell's borrowed impulse of the image of contemporary postmodern Japan unfolds in a complex plot densely saturated with media images and popular culture scenes. It is clear that Mitchell's dialogue with

Murakami largely reflects the English author's innovations in regard to the representation of Japan. On the one hand, Mitchell picks the most important – a new image of Japan, which is an alternative to the Orientalist vision of the nineteenth century – as an image of his favourite country where he lived for a long time.

1.4 Intertextuality, Literary Influences and the Image of Japan in the Works of Murakami Haruki and David Mitchell

Here the focus is on the literal connections between the works of Murakami and Mitchell and the peculiarity of their visions of Japan. I would like to start with the example of intertextuality related to the music motif to provide a general idea of the links between the two authors.

It is well known that Murakami's works are somewhat musical both in their text structure (such as rhythm) and depiction of musical compositions in the text. The names of many works of Murakami are the names of famous pop songs: 『ノルウェイ森』 (*Norwegian Wood*, a famous song of *The Beatles*). 『1963/1982年のイパネマ娘』 (*Girl from Ipanema 1963 / 1982*) is a reference to the famous Bossanova, *The Girl from Ipanema*. The first part of the name of the famous novel 『国境の南,太陽の西』 (*South of the Border, West of the Sun*) is also a well-known song, "South of the Border", which glorifies such singers as Jean Autry and Frank Sinatra. 『ダンス・ダンス・ダンス』 (*Dance, Dance, Dance*) – such bands as *Beach Boys* and *The Dell* sand the song with the same name.

Chapter "Tokyo" in Mitchel's *Ghostwritten* is built around a character named Satoru who perceives the world the same way Murakami's characters do, through jazz and Western pop music. For instance, in Murakami's novel *Dance Dance Dance*, we find music references in abundance. I intentionally offer this quote, which was translated into English as a much shorter version of the original:

> I put his body in a Seiyu supermarket bag, placed him on the backseat of the car, and drove to the hardware store for a shovel. I turned off the highway a good ways up in the hills and found an appropriate grove of trees. A fair distance back from the road I dug a hole one meter deep and laid Kipper in his shopping bag to rest. Then I shoveled dirt on top of him. Sorry, I told the little guy, that's just how it goes. Birds were singing the whole time I was burying him. The upper registers of a flute recital. Once the hole was filled in, I tossed the shovel into the trunk of the car, and got back on the highway. I turned the radio on as I drove home to Tokyo.
> Which is when the DJ had to put on Ray Charles moan-ing about being born to lose ... and now I'm losing you (Murakami 2010a, p. 10).

Or in *Norwegian Wood* there are lines like this:

> The Kinokuniya bookstore was as jam-packed as a rush-hour train. I bought a copy of Faulkner's Light in August and went to the noisiest jazz café I could think of, reading my new book while listening to Ornette Coleman and Bud Powell and drinking hot, thick, foul-tasting coffee (Murakami 2010b, p. 199).

The music references are numerous in Murakami's novels, and it would be difficult to list them all. However, these two quotes easily illustrate the author's attitude towards Western culture in general and music in particular.

Similarly, Satoru goes through his day constantly thinking of it in jazz terms: "Static hisses on telephone lines. Jimmy Cobb's percussion on 'Blue in Green'", "I felt in a Billie Holiday mood", "It was a Mal Waldron time of day. (…) Every note of 'Left Alone' fell, a drop of lead into a deep well. Jackie McLean's saxophone circled in the air, so sad it could barely leave the ground", and "It was a morning for Ella Fitzgerald" (Mitchell 2008, p.17). Such a technique of representation of Japan through popular Western musical compositions is an artistic innovation of Mitchell, who is willing to open a new aesthetical channel of seeing Japan, to look at it differently, destroying the formed stereotypes of the famous dichotomy "East is East, and West is West"[2], making the image of the Other closer. Here we can witness the representation of modern Japan in terms of Western music, which creates an image of a Westernised country under the undeniable influence of America.

In order to expand the range of the representation of modern Japan, I focus on Mitchell's "Japanese" novels, which have the greatest and most easily detectable links to Murakami's works. Those novels are *Ghostwritten* (1999) and *Number9Dream* (2001), and I am going to base my analysis on them, demonstrating, where it is possible, the influences of Murakami or the difference between the two authors, especially in regard to the image of Japan.

Ghostwritten (1999) can be interpreted as a kind of artistic imagological experiment. The central theme of the work is the representation of non-Western nations and ethnic groups. It exposes Orientalist stereotypes and attempts to withdraw from ethnocentric clichés in portraying the world as a "global village"[3] where the barriers between different nations and cultures gradually

---

[2] A line from the poem 'The Ballad of East and West' by Rudyard Kipling (2021).

[3] 'Global village' is a term introduced by Marshall McLuhan, popularized in his books *The Gutenberg Galaxy: The Making of Typographic Man* (1962) and *Understanding Media* (1973). McLuhan described how the globe has been turned into a village by technology,

disappear. Hugo Dyserinck, a Belgian philologist and specialist in literature famous for his imagological studies, emphasises the importance of analysing the post-ethnic and post-national models: "Imagology should also investigate the possibility of developing – in literature and its surrounding field - post-national identity models" (Dyserinck 2003, p. 6). In his first novel, Mitchell undertakes this task in a literary form, investigating the possibilities of representing the Other without going back to stereotypical ethno-centred thinking.

Mitchell's *Ghostwritten* consists of nine interconnected stories ("Okinawa", "Tokyo", "Hong Kong", "Holy Mountain", "Mongolia", "Petersburg", "London", "Clear Island", "Night Train"). Each of them has its own narrator, and the events take place in different countries. The epilogue ("Underground") returns the reader to the first chapter. In an interview with McWeeney, Mitchell explains that

> the first three stories started life as unrelated short stories that I wrote on location. Then when I realized there was narrative potential waiting to be tapped by linking the stories, it made sense to keep the locations on the move. The far-flung locations test-drive this interconnected novel about interconnection more strenuously (Mitchell 2011, para. 15).

In this way, it was the author's intention to keep his novel "off-centre" and "on the move", showing the kaleidoscope of cultures and values, never favouring any of them.

Although some chapters of *Ghostwritten* are set in such centres of Western culture and economy as London and New York, most of the events in the novel are concentrated in countries traditionally perceived by Western cultural consciousness as Other and mystical, mysterious, unidentified – Japan, Hong Kong, China, Mongolia and Russia. Thus, the work of Mitchell is a multi-layered phenomenon of interconnected narratives and subjectivities that constantly overlap and are absorbed by one another. The themes that combine different characters and different scenes are the following: the role of chance, guilt, responsibility, and apocalyptic motif. As one of the characters of the novel states, "We drift, often on a whim, searching for something to search for" (Mitchell 2008, p. 153), and this search (which every now and then proves to be useless) includes looking for one's identity as well as for sustainable features of national character.

The topic of Japan was further developed by Mitchell in his second novel *Number9Dream* (2001). Peter Childs and John Green, outlining Bakhtin's theory

---

making it possible the instantaneous movement of information from every quarter to every point at the same time.

of dialogism (1979), argue that *Number9Dream* is "a palimpsest of competing voices and styles that cycle through disparate but always interlinked temporal and spatial settings" (Childs and Green 2011, p. 26), which are always related to the search for identity. Thus, we can see the author continues to develop the topic he started in his previous novel. To work on this eternal theme, Mitchell chooses Japan and writes the novel on behalf of a local resident because, as he expresses in an online interview, "using Japanese protagonists seems to be a more convincing way to go about that" (Mitchell 2014, para. 17). This means that in order to explore the Japanese identity and the notion of Japaneseness, for Mitchell, it was easier to perform taking on a Japanese perspective through his Japanese characters, rather than introduce a Western character and represent Japan through his/her eyes.

The plot of *Number9Dream* builds around the search of a young Japanese guy, Miyake Eiji, for his father. Eiji comes from the distant rural provincial island of Yakushima and is intended to find his parent in the big postmodern, post-industrial city of Tokyo. The novel picks up and develops themes commonly found in classic coming-of-age novels or *Bildungsroman*. Kate Simpson goes as far as to call it a "postmodern *Bildungsroman*" that "questions the viability of the conventional coming-of-age quest or self-knowledge in a postmodern, late capitalist context while simultaneously tantalizing the reader with this possibility" (Simpson 2011, p. 51). Against this background, an eventful plot unfolds where the real adventures of a hero are skilfully interwoven with fantasies, dreams, memories, hallucinations, and so on. And it is not possible on the spot to distinguish one from another. As O'Donnell calls it, "*Number9Dream* is a hallucinatory journey through late-twentieth-century Japanese urban culture" (O'Donnell 2015, p. 51). Notably, fantasies dominate the protagonist's thoughts, and he always retreats into them. For instance, it is noticeable in the episode when in his imagination, Eiji goes to see his father's lawyer, but in reality, he never does, having not mustered the courage to do so. However, the end of the novel shows how reality can cruelly interfere with such fantasies.

The ending of the novel would be predictable in a mythological way: the hero comes back to the sources, back to the native island; however, the open ending of the book is deliberately unconventional. Upon hearing the terrible message about the earthquake in Tokyo, Eiji stands up and starts to run. The last – the ninth – chapter presents a blank page; the author gives the readers the opportunity to finish it on their own.

In his works, Mitchell creates certain images which can be considered exoticisms; however, I will try to show that the writer uses them in a very particular way. It is also important to trace intertextual connections to Murakami and other writers. First of all, it is necessary to underline that, unlike Murakami, whose leading feature of the creative method is the so-called

Westernization of the text and displaying of the Japanese flavour without using traditional symbols of Japanese culture, Mitchell does not give up his exotic view on the country, but translates this implanted strangeness into his own radically different language, turning the stereotype of traditional Japaneseness into extreme parodies.

Mitchell's protagonist in chapter "Tokyo", the novel *Ghostwritten,* can be viewed as a direct analogy of the character of Murakami's works – Boku (which means "I" in Japanese). The narration in the mentioned chapter, as in most of Murakami's works, is in the first person. Thus, the English writer constructs dialogical subtext to the mentioned chapter. Satoru, the protagonist, knows little about whom he wants to be but is definitely aware of whom he does not want to be, which is why he is trying to fall out of the system. After school, he takes no exams and goes to work in a record store. Murakami's characters behave rather similarly. For instance, Tamura Kafka from the novel *Kafka on the Shore* (2006) is a turbulent teenager who drops out of school; Okada Toru from *The Wind-Up Bird Chronicle* (2010) leaves a law firm where he used to work; Takahashi Tetsuya from *After Dark* (2007) is a law student, who cannot imagine himself as an employee of the big company. Satoru also cannot find his place in this big world, but he admires jazz, watches old movies with Humphrey Bogart, enjoys Western literature and has no specific goal in life.

However, in the architectonics of the images of Mitchell's Satoru and Murakami's Boku also can find a few differences, both insignificant and impressive, which proves the originality of perspective in the works of Mitchell. Thus, in contrast to Murakami's Americanized Japanese protagonists, who usually drink beer and coffee, Satoru starts his mornings with tea, and the author takes the most deliberate and almost ironic clarification: " n entirely ordinary morning. Time for oolong tea" (Mitchell 2008, p. 35) as if intentionally yet jokingly emphasising Oriental identity of his protagonist. An even more impressive distinguishing feature of the image of Satoru is his nationality. In Murakami's works, despite all the diversity of national entries in his text (Western brands and names, music, books, Asian (non-Japanese) characters), the protagonist Boku is always a thoroughbred Japanese. The main reason for his concern is only a territorial origin: most of Murakami's characters, as the author himself, come from the Kansai area and then move to Tokyo, where they start feeling estranged. Murakami problematizes the semantics of feelings of Self-Other, depicting that strangers can be perceived not only as non-Japanese but the Japanese themselves in their native country and that this category is related to the inside of the "self".

Mitchell's text also deploys this motif of regional differences in Japan. However, if those can be viewed as cultural barriers in Murakami's novels, Mitchell raises them to the level of stereotype, ironically depicting the geographical and cultural dichotomies. Thus, one of the clients of the record store where

Satoru works is the editor Fujimoto who returns to Tokyo from a trip to Kyoto and buys some records one day. He points out: "Oh, Kyoto was Kyoto. Temples and shrines, meetings with printers. Uppity shopkeepers who think they have a monopoly on manners. It's good to be back. Once a Tokyoite, always a Tokyoite" (Mitchell 2008, p. 60). In this way, the widespread rivalry of Tokyo-Kyoto (Kansai-Kanto regions) is represented, showing how people from Tokyo think people from Kyoto are uppity, more traditional and conservative. Murakami, Kansai-born himself, also represents a similar theme in his works when his characters come to Tokyo (Kanto) from the Kansai area; however, he does not go as far as to make jokes. This alienation is, to some extent, comparable to the alienation of a foreigner in a foreign country, but this comparison is not entirely appropriate.

As I mentioned before, Murakami's Boku is always Japanese, but Mitchell goes further in his literary and imagological experiment. Satoru is a "pure" Japanese only according to the documents but is actually half-Japanese on his father's side: Satoru's mother was a Filipina, expelled from the country. Satoru was brought up by Mama-san in one of the hostess clubs and, through influential friends of his foster mother, received full Japanese citizenship. In this situation of alienation in their own country, the nationalist image of Japan is modified, pointing out the image of the so-called monoethnic Japanese nation. This issue is examined in every detail in the study *Multiethnic Japan* by John Lie (2004). Satoru's non-Japanese background affects his fate, for people always find the truth: "It was as tough as having Korean parents. People find out. Gossip works telepathically in Tokyo. The city is vast, but there's always someone who knows someone whom someone knows" (Mitchell 2008, p. 44). The rumours about his non-Japanese background come up during his school years, causing Satoru to be bullied at times, which is just another feature of the education system in Japan and is rather important for the recreation of a socio-cultural image of the country.

Based on all the above, it is possible to say that the image of Mitchell's Satoru has various connections to Murakami's Boku: on the music level, regional level or his general attitudes to the Western culture. In this sense, Satoru is a kind of complicated pastiche. In the postmodernist interpretation of Ihab Hassan (1987), Fredric Jameson (1993) and others, pastiche is defined as a collision in an intertextual space of two or more pieces of content and stylistically different textual worlds. Thus, there quasi parodying effect can be found, in which each piece of irony overcomes all others and, in turn, is ironically overcome by each of them. The intertextual relationship of Mitchell with the artistic technique of creating images in Murakami's work is manifested here most clearly. Satoru, this character-pastiche feels his difficult existence, and this feeling is reflected in his thoughts: "For a moment I had an odd sensation of being in a story that someone was writing, but soon that sensation too was being swallowed up" (Mitchell 2008, p. 45). In fact, this passage is bidirectional, for it is not just about Satoru, who thinks himself to be a book character, but also it hints at the "author" himself, the Ghostwriter (as the name of the novel is *Ghostwritten*), who "writes" these "biographies" given in the novel. On the other hand, Eiji, the hero of the *Number9Dream*, concludes that "Reality is the page. Life is the word" (Mitchell 2001, p. 267), and this remark may as well be an echo of poststructuralist theories of modern culture. Satoru's and Eiji's words are a sign of the entering of Murakami's citations in Mitchell's text inscribed in a broad cultural context of today. Thus, Okada Toru of *The Wind-Up Bird Chronicle* by Murakami also thinks of himself as a literary character, even implausible, "I felt as if I had become part of a badly written novel" (Murakami 2010c, p. 181). From the given quotations, it is clear that both authors create their characters within the text space, being aware of the contemporary postmodern literary theories, and that Mitchell also uses this to strengthen his link to Murakami's texts. The disappearing line between reality and pseudo-reality of the human existence and its connection to a literary text was once outlined in the famous play by Luigi Pirandello, *Six Characters in Search of an Author* (2016). This postmodern game with the reader comes in the mentioned passages of both authors; however, in Mitchell's works, it is also a deliberate component of polyvalent quotations as an important component of the images of Satoru and Eiji, which involves not only Murakami's works but Gustave Flaubert, Jerome David Salinger and the others.

Another important motif in Mitchell's works is the protagonist's search for his roots. In this, we can trace a topic important for the literary context of the twentieth and early twenty-first-century: the problematisation of one's own identity, including national identity as well. Mitchell's technique of artistic reverse in textual modelling of the consciousness of a modern Japanese person is the main strategy of representing of auto-image of Japan in his works. Satoru does not know his father; his mother was expelled from the country. Satoru never saw him; there was only a random encounter with a stranger who came to the shop and in whom Satoru "saw himself" for a moment and guessed that this man could have been his father. The lack of a father figure confuses the character much more than the absence of the mother. Starting from his first novel, Mitchell resorts to this type of male character that Kate Simpson (2011) calls "surrogate father". Thus, the role of father for Satoru to a varying degree is performed by the following characters: Taro, a bouncer in a hostess club who several times literally saved the boy's life; Fujimoto, an editor in a publishing house, who constantly provides Satoru with books in exchange for Satoru's advice on jazz.

The motifs of "father" as well as "father search" receive their maximum development in Mitchell's second novel *Number9Dream* (2001). The main character is looking for his father throughout the whole novel, and along the way, he gets to meet the leader of the Yakuza, his own grandfather on the paternal side, and Buntaro, his landlord. To some extent, all of them replace him as the father figure, highlighting different facets of the image of modern Japan. In Mitchell's third novel, *Cloud Atlas* (2004), we can also find the implementation of a topic: Robert Frobisher, a musician from a good family, who was deprived of parental recognition and heritage, finds a new home (and the symbolic father-teacher) in Belgium in a family of a famous but old and sick composer. From this, it can be understood that for Mitchell, this "father" topic is not accidental since he actualizes it in a number of his books.

It should be noted that this motif of the search for fatherhood does not acquire such a deep development in Murakami's works, though it is present in the novels *The Wind-Up Bird Chronicle* (2010), *Dance, Dance, Dance* (2010), *After Dark* (2007), *Kafka on the Shore* (2006), and *1Q84* (2013). In his avoidance of the topic of family ties, the deterioration of family relationships in Japan is reflected. As a result, instead of searching for family happiness, Murakami's characters flee their houses and kill their parents (like in *Kafka on the Shore*) or beat their wives and abuse their sisters (as in *1Q84*). In Mitchell's *Ghostwritten*, especially in chapter "Tokyo", this motif of fatherhood is also revealed as the inability and impossibility of the characters (father and son) to meet. Satoru realizes that his father must be from a good and rich family if, in 18 years (since the time Satoru was born), he was able to "to clean up the stink of such a scandal" (Mitchell 2008, p. 39) as he was a patron of hostess bars. As mentioned earlier, Satoru is sure that he once saw his father. In one of the random visitors of the store where he works, Satoru "recognises himself": "I knew I recognised him from somewhere, but I thought he was a musician. He looked around the shop and asked for a Chick-Corea recording that we happened to have. He bought it, I wrapped it for him, and he left. Only afterwards did I realise that he reminded me of me" (Mitchell 2008, p. 56). Reflecting on this, Satoru comes to the conclusion that such a coincidence is impossible in a city like Tokyo and that his father came to buy a record in order to take a look at his son.

Mitchell creates a similar situation in his second novel, *Number9Dream*. On a sleepless night, Eiji receives a phone call from a man ordering a pizza with some really weird ingredients in it. As it turns out, the man is Eiji's father, and this motif of fortuitousness is brought up in such a description of events. The father figure is also created with all its specifics: he knows about his son's existence and consciously rejects him and yet, just for fun and out of curiosity, comes to look at his offspring (in *Ghostwritten*) or calls him on the phone to discuss unusual pizza choices.

In the deployment of the family theme, we can see much in common with Murakami's novels, although stylistically, Mitchell's works, if compared to the "deadpan" style of the Japanese author, are imbued with lyricism. It can be seen in the image of the cat in the novel *Number9Dream*, the character's feelings about her possible death, establishing relationships with his mother, and the image of his deceased twin sister Anju and warm relationship with the landlord and all his family. Eiji's search for a national and cultural identity manifested in the theme of fatherhood, ends up in his refusal to meet with his biological father. As O'Donnell points out, "the logic of the classic Bildungsroman would dictate that, after numerous external and internal divagations and false leads, his quest would end in a paternal acknowledgement that would equalize the loss of his twin sister (effectively, a loss of the self) with the relocation of Eiji's identity in the generational symbolic order" (O'Donnell 2015, p. 55). When he, at last, meets Daisuke Tsukiyama, though, he decides against identifying himself. Thus, this final loss of interest in his roots indicates the deconstruction of one of the important topics in the literature of the twentieth century, the problem of self-search[4]. The fact, which constitutes the main law of human existence for his grandfather, however, does not lose its meaning for Eiji as well: "Bloodlines are the stuff of life. Of identity!" (Mitchell 2001, p. 274). While searching for his father, Eiji learns about himself and his family that he never met (the family of "samurai" kamikaze-pilot Subaru Tsukiyama), and decides after long hesitation to re-establish his relationship with his mother, who, unlike Daisuke Tsukiyama, wants to get closer to her son, though once he was nearly killed by her.

Eiji reflects on the history of his country, questioning the legality and reasons for the war, which involved his great-grandfather Subaru Tsukiyama. He asks himself if Subaru gave his life for this Japan, which came into existence after World War II, but he never diminishes the heroism of his relative. On his return home, he reads Subaru's diaries on his sister's empty grave (the real grave for drowned Anju[5], as for Subaru, was the ocean itself). Thus, not Japaneseness but humanity is the defining feature of Mitchell's character. As Holden Caulfield

---

[4] This problem in the context of the twentieth century literature was thoroughly studied, among others, by Ihab Hassan, particularly in his paper 'Quest for the Subject: The Self in Literature' (1998); Jean-François Lyotard in *The Postmodern Condition: A Report on Knowledge* (1984); Jean Baudrillard in *Simulacra and Simulation* (1994) and *The Illusion of the End* (1994); Gerhard Hoffmann in *From Modernism to Postmodernism. Concepts and Strategies of Postmodern American Fiction* (2005).

[5] The name of Mitchell's character, Anju, who drowned in the lake, can be another reference to the Japanese literature – *Sansho the Bailiff* [Snasho Dayuu], a short story by Mori Ogai about a brother and a sister, at the end of which the sister (named Anju) commits suicide by walking into a lake.

in Salinger's *The Cather in the Rye* (1951) feels gently for his sister Phoebe, Mitchell's character Eiji loves his sister Anju, and the feelings of pain and loss are what establish the basis of his humanity, rather than his exclusive Japaneseness of "flesh and blood".

Another component of the image of Japan in the novels of Murakami and Mitchell is defined by the attitude of Japanese people to foreigners. The first foreigner to appear in the chapter "Tokyo" in *Ghostwritten* is the first buyer of the week in the store of music records where Satoru works. The Japanese character finds it rather difficult to comprehend where the foreigner is from: Europe, America or Australia. And here, we see the example of Satoru's stereotypical thinking: "You can never tell because they all look the same. A lanky, zitty foreigner" (Mitchell 2008, p. 35). Here can be found some bias towards Europeans and Americans. Furthermore, although Satoru notices the visitor's knowledge of jazz and his professional approach to record search, his friendly attitude toward the foreigner immediately changes when he notices the foreigner's lack of Japanese language skills: "I asked him where he was from. He said thank you very much. Westerners can't learn Japanese" (Mitchell 2008, p. 35). As many researchers point out, this stereotype is extremely common among the Japanese. Koichi Iwabuchi (1994, 2002) indicates that there is a belief among the Japanese that only Japanese can understand Japanese themselves. Exactly in this way, another character of the novel, Fujimoto, stresses the attitude of the Japanese to the cherry blossom:

> The last of the cherry blossom. On the tree, it turns ever more perfect. And when it's perfect, it falls. And then of course once it hits the ground it gets all mushed up. So it's only absolutely perfect when it's falling through the air, this way and that, for the briefest time... I think that only we Japanese can really understand that, don't you? (Mitchell 2008, p. 36).

Coming from a Japanese person, who is a character in the English novel, it sounds rather ironic.

In a subtly mocking way, Mitchell represents a stereotypical image of Japanese uniqueness formed in Western culture. In *Number9Dream* we can find another proof for such a view. The basis for this particular case of parody may be found in Basho's famous haiku about the pond and the frog: "Old pond — frogs jumped in — sound of water"[6], which is associatively linked to the situation in the novel where two Japanese are admiring the rain and the puddles: "Circles are born, while circles born a second ago live. Circles live, while circles living a second ago die. Circles die, while new circles are born"

---

[6] 古池や蛙飛こむ水のおと (芭蕉, 2013)

(Mitchell 2001, p. 287). These are the words that appear in the diary of Subaru Tsukiyama, great-grandfather of Eiji, and here, in particular, he describes the aesthetic discussion between himself and his colleague Kusakabe. This image of Kusakabe, the bearer of the traditional Japanese worldview, though episodic, is opposed to the image of the lieutenant, who also positions himself as a representative of Japan as a traditional nation. However, unlike Kusakabe's aesthetic aspirations, the lieutenant actualises the "samurai spirit", which is in unison with the spirit of the time described (World War II), causing constant culturally and ideologically loaded clashes between the lieutenant and Kusakabe. The irony of the scene where Subaru and Kusakabe contemplate puddles is multiplied by Subaru's earnest and serious commentary that Kusakabe should have been born a wandering poet-priest, to which Kusakabe replies that he may have been once.

Significantly, in the works of Murakami, aesthetic Japaneseness, even in its ironic way, does not reveal itself and, thus, serves more of a deliberate "minus-technique"[7], although the emphasis on such "de-anesthetization" of Japaneseness is not uncommon in the works of modern non-Japanese authors who write about Japan. For instance, the English writer Iain Banks, very much like Mitchell, is drawn to the image of cherry blossoms, as well as the traditional image of Fuji, when he constructs an image of Japanese women in his novel *Canal Dreams* (1989): "Fuji invisible for weeks then suddenly there, floating on a sea of cloud, a flurry of cherry blossoms lasting hardly longer than a pink snowstorm ... all seemed to conspire to sweep her life away from under her" (Banks 2008, p. 36). This concentration in the same sentence of several exotic stereotypical images of Japan (Fuji and cherry blossoms) has the effect of ironic intent. This Japanese image of Fuji, along with the European image of the cello (the character is an outstanding musician), haunts Banks's character every time she recollects her childhood and Japan she left. In the novel, the protagonist brings her old, heavily damaged cello to the mountain Fuji from where she observes the blooming: "Cherry blossom painted the Tokyo parks pink" (Banks 2008, p. 37). And then she sets the cello on fire: "The cello groaned and creaked and popped as it died, and the strings snapped like whips. The flames and smoke looked pale and insubstantial against the budding trees and the bright sky, but the heated fumes, rising through the clear fresh air of spring, made Fuji itself tremble" (Banks 2008, p. 39). The author stresses that it was spring, and the sound of the burning cello creates a volatile and smoky image of Fuji, which

---

[7] The term was suggested by the semiotician Yuri Lotman (Лотман 1998), who also came up with another term "significant absence" to describe artistic forms, which miss some detail

refers to the artistic techniques of Hokusai (tradition of Ukiyo-e, "pictures of the floating world").

Fuji and cherry blossom in Banks's novel are depicted as a part of the life of the heroine and as a stereotype as well, a sort of decorative addition to the spirit of Japaneseness in the novel. In contrast to these representations, Mitchell's images appear more ironic, as mentioned earlier. By introducing some stereotypes (such as cherry blossoms) into his text, the author at once playfully destroys it by saying: "I think that only we Japanese can really understand that, don't you?" (Mitchell 2008, p. 36).

Unlike Mitchell, Murakami intentionally avoids the ironic representation of the unique Japanese aesthetic worldview. His characters are modern Japanese, who are not all that different from Western people. Apart from the distinctively Japanese names, Murakami's books lack representations of the specific Japanese aesthetics, which can be found in the works of such "distinctively" Japanese writers as Kawabata Yasunari and Tanizaki Jun'ichiro. Murakami sees and writes about Americanized Japan, where there is no place for the old values and images.

Another problematic topic – stereotypical attitudes of Japanese to foreigners and notions of Japanese uniqueness – can be found in Mitchell's novel *Ghostwritten*. Satoru, Mithell's character, openly shows his disgust with the Western way of relaxation. He thinks to himself, for instance: "I've seen foreigners get drunk in bars out in Shibuya and places, and they turn into animals. Japanese people never do that" (Mitchell 2008, p. 61). The apparent contrast between the "purity" of the Japanese and the "dirt" of the Europeans fits into a standard image of the West and Westerners in the eyes of the Japanese. Mitchell intentionally reinforces this kind of stereotypical image of Japan regarding foreigners. Murakami, on the other hand, seems to avoid writing on this topic: his characters speak with anyone freely. In his first novel, *Hear the Wind Sing* (1979), the bartender Jay, a Chinese, even says: "But we are all brothers after all" ["でもみんな兄弟さ"] (Murakami 2004, p. 102). However, it is worth noting that the historical connotations, that is, Japan's aggressive war in China and atrocities on the continent, mark Murakami's novels and shape his specific attitude toward China.

The problem of intercultural communication in Mitchell's work is manifested through the representation of Satoru and his friend Koji who meet with two girls from Scotland. Satoru's first impression of them is as follows: "I just assumed they were English teachers at some crappy English school, but they turned out to be 'exotic dancers'" (Mitchell 2008, p. 65). Satoru cannot directly communicate with the girls, for as the Japanese language seems impossible for foreigners to study, the English language appears to be so for the Japanese. Moreover, Satoru observes: "English being a girl's subject, I didn't study it much" (Mitchell 2008, p. 65). Koji performs the role of the interpreter in their conversation with the girls. The next problem is manifested in their conversation about the difference in the behaviour of young girls in Scotland (the West) and Japan. The Scottish girls note that all girls in Scotland are trying to be different from each other. In Japan, the situation is the opposite, which always strikes Satoru, for he notices it even when his Chinese friend enters his shop along with Japanese girls. At this particular moment, Satoru thinks to himself, "They were pretty, I guess, but they were all clones of the same ova. Their hair was the same length, their lipstick the same colour, their bodies curving in the same way beneath their same uniform" (Mitchell 2008, p. 60). Such cultural differences and peculiarities form "a whole way of life",[8] which is also part of the complicated and multi-layered image of modern Japan observed by Mitchell.

In that way, the English author represents Japanese national and cultural stereotypes through the point of view of the other nation, creating a certain hetero-image of the country, and then he proves it through the opinions of his Japanese character, creating the auto-image of Japan as well. In such a complicated way of representing Japan in his novels, Mitchell emphasises the conventional nature of the "Self-Other" dichotomy. In this sense, the concept of nationality itself looks in Mitchell's work more like a certain convention and/or a social construct.

Another topic of the intercultural dialogue in Mitchell's *Ghostwritten* is the question of imitation of American culture as a form of protest against the Japanese tradition, especially among young people. Satoru feels confused and is not sure that he can explain it to the girls, so he just thinks to himself:

> I wanted to say that it's not America they're aping, it's the Japan of their parents that they're rejecting. And since there's no home-grown counterculture, they just take hold of the nearest one to hand, which happens to be American. But it's not American culture exploiting us. It's us exploiting it (Mitchell 2008, p. 65).

In such a way, a very intricate topic is introduced. It is the discourse of national identity in the context of globalization and the clash of cultures. Mitchell implicitly asks here who benefits more, the influencing culture or the culture that is under the influence.

From the conducted analysis, we can conclude that Mitchell offers an imagological vision of the national and cultural identity of contemporary Japan

---

[8] The famous phrase is coined by Raymond Williams (2017), the leading thinker in the field of cultural studies.

and joins the discourse of a cross-cultural phenomenon of the image of modern Japan. The absence of the counterculture and the borrowing of other peoples' traditions can explain, as both the author and his character think, the ambiguity of the image of modern Japan. This image shows that although Americanness is not a desirable ideal, it is a means to overcome the tradition of stringent regulations in the family, society and morality. It is also significant how the mentioned conversation ends. All of a sudden, the American boyfriends of the girls from Scotland make their appearance, and Satoru calls them "bloody great US marine gorillas" (Mitchell 2008, p. 65). The general attitude of the Japanese toward Americans determines this playful remark and makes it another facet in a kaleidoscope of imagological observations on Japan by the English writer.

1.5 Conclusion

The extended and diverse imagological specification of the image of Japan (such as Fuji and cherry blossoms, Japanese bars, attitudes toward foreigners, etc.) defines the modern image of the country, opposing the stereotypical image of distant exotic East, which representation as a cultural universal, prevails in Western literature of the previous period. Therefore, the comparative analysis of the "Japanese" novels of the English writer (*Ghostwritten* and *Number9Dream*) as well as works of Murakami Haruki (*A Wild Sheep Chase, The Wind-Up Bird Chronicle, Hard-Boiled Wonderland and the End of the World* and so on) reveal the range of problems involving the dichotomies of East vs West, Tokyo vs Kyoto, small provincial town vs big post-industrial city, and show how the writers construct images of Japan from the viewpoint of both foreigners and Japanese themselves. The whole set of various ideas and stereotypes about the Japanese, Europeans and Americans is embodied in the texts of Mitchell and Murakami and consequently deconstructed. This narrative strategy is crucial in the representation of the modern complexity of intercultural contacts and historical memory as the basis of misunderstandings that arise during the transcultural dialogue.

So far, I have given examples of common points between Mitchell's and Murakami's work. One of the characteristics of Murakami's fiction, apart from being "deadpan" and lacking emotion/sentimentalism, is, on a certain level, being "mimetic". For instance, Murakami describes bored people to represent modern Japan and simultaneously share the atmosphere with the reader. In addition, as mentioned earlier, Murakami writes about jazz and other Western music in his fiction to represent the modern reality of Japan, where people do prefer those genres to Japanese *enka* and *min'you*. Of course, it is not limited only to music since many Japanese consume Western genres and brands in all spheres of culture. It is quite striking that, being a Japanese himself, Murakami does not use stereotypical icons of Japaneseness. More specifically, Murakami recreates in his writing the real atmosphere of modern Japan, something resonant to the reader, in order to represent Japan.

Mitchell, on the other hand, inspired by Murakami in many ways, preserves his creative individuality and does not try to avoid stereotypes in his novels. However, he uses them playfully, in a postmodern ironic and parodic fashion, deconstructing them by doing so. Thus, the image of Japan is represented in Mitchell's novels as a complex dialogue with the artistic representation of Japaneseness in the novels of Murakami. The authors share the feature of the accentuation of cultural and historical changes regarding the views on Japan and Japaneseness, their refusal to follow cultural and ethnocentric concepts, developed long ago. Creating the image of Japan with a close connection to Murakami texts, Mitchell emphasises his position of perceiving both Japan and the world as an uncomfortable place of human existence. In the works of both of the authors, not only is revealed the question of what it means to be Japanese in the modern globalised world, but also what it means to be human.

Chapter 2
The Concept of Techno-Orientalism and Techno-Images of Japan in the Works of Murakami Haruki and David Mitchell

2.1 Perceptions of Japan through Different Types of Orientalism

Having established the intertextual links between Murakami's and Mitchell's works, I am going to study the image of Japan in their novels from the orientalist and, more specifically, techno-orientalist perspective. There is no denying that Orientalism played a crucial part in causing all sorts of cross-cultural conflicts when it comes to ever-so-complicated relations between East and West. The main reason for that is generally considered the interpretation of the other culture from the perspective of one's own cultural values (mostly Western). Japan, being an Asian country, is not excluded. However, in this chapter, I attempt to prove that this kind of perception and representation does have its own specifics, and the process or "orientalization" may be different in many regards from its neighbouring countries. Here, in the following subchapters, I look into the concept of orientalism, described by Edward Said (1979, 1993), and point out the Japanese application of it (2.1.1); analyse such peculiar phenomena as "self-orientalization" (2.1.2) and "techno-orientalism" (2.1.3). After that, in subchapters 2.1 and 2.2, I explore how Murakami and Mitchell address the concept of orientalism and techno-orientalism in their literary texts and look into the similarities and differences in their respective standpoints.

2.1.1 Orientalism

During the twentieth century, Japan expanded its influence in all areas of cultural and economic activities. Because of globalisation and transcultural interactions, the system of signs called "Japan" was formed, in terms of Roland Barthes (1983). Because of the variety of possible meanings, it becomes increasingly difficult to identify or correlate the image of Japan with a specific phenomenon. The image of this country in different types of art, including literature, is surrounded by orientalist stereotypes, which, as indicated by Edward Said, are mostly based on cultural biases, especially within Europe and North America (Said 1979). It was noted that there are a few different kinds of orientalist discourse on Japan, and orientalism and techno-orientalism are the most popular among them (Lozano-Mendez 2010; Posadas 2011; Said 1993). Within these concepts, the West speaks for the Other (non-West), not allowing it to speak for itself. However, the discourse on "otherness" in Japan has its own specifics, such as self-orientalisation, because, as known, the country internalised at some level Western orientalist discourse and identifies now its own identity through it (Iwabuchi 1994, 2002; Wagenaar 2016). Here I will focus on these concepts, starting with how Orientalism relates to Japan.

As Steven Rosen points out, "Interpretations of Japan, as well as other Asian cultures, often carries an implicit assumption that the West is rational (and superior), whereas the East is bound by ancient traditions (and is inferior)" (Rosen 2000, p. 15). This point of view is derived directly from the concept of Orientalism, which has long been associated with a particular form of stereotypical Western visions of Asia. Understandably, such an approach can bring about certain problems since any communication is impossible when the other culture is perceived as completely Other. Nowadays, it is important to overcome straight dichotomies, which divide the world into "us" versus "them". That is why in academic fields, the ideas about transcending or overcoming Orientalism have emerged. It was noticed that Western cultures often project onto Japan a lot of stereotypes, among which the most popular are those that regard Japan as "a monolithic culture which is excessively authoritarian, hierarchical, and patriarchal" (Rosen 2000, p. 15), which may bear some truth in itself but does not cover the whole truth.

Orientalism is often accompanied by a version of ethnocentrism, which is understood as "the interpretation and evaluation of others through this epistemological screen, with the implicit assumption that one's own mode of understanding is superior because it is invariantly true" (Erchak 1992, p. 90). Orientalism, thus, is a cultural myth based on a Western worldview, which, according to Said, "includes a battery of desires, repressions, investments and projections" (Said 1993, p. 90). In cultural texts and narratives, including literature, orientalism manifests through certain metaphors, which usually depict the East as strange and exotic and underline its otherness. The East – or Orient – here stands for all the varieties of non-Western cultures, being a single simplified and mystified image and an enormous generalization.

Researchers repeatedly point out that Western and especially American stereotypes and images of China and Chinese people are generally kinder than those of Japan (Johnson 2001; Rosen 2000). That may indicate that the image of China is considered closer, more understandable and perhaps less threatening. Rosen offers such characteristics about Chinese people: "frank and direct, individualistic, rational, educated, pragmatic and practical" (Rosen 2000, pp. 15-16). Japan, on the other hand, is "the last other to be discovered" (Rosen 2000). Rosen describes Japan as follows: "Japanese social institutions signify

Japan to be a culture with a high level of sophistication in Western eyes, yet it also appears as highly feudal and totally anachronistic to the moral imperatives of the modern world; the culture as a whole tends to be quite opaque to us – Japanese cultural mores are exotic, quixotic and even absurd" (Rosen 2000, pp. 15-16). Of course, there are also "positive" stereotypical images of Japan in the West, which mostly present the highly exotic, sophisticated, mystified and romanticized country. Some of those images, especially the ones regarding mystical ties to nature, are very popular among the Japanese themselves. Still, stereotypical visions usually have their hidden agendas, and by making something seem exotic, it is easier to distance from it and regard it as the cultural "other".

The academic study of Japan in the West started with the famous book by Ruth Benedict, *Chrysanthemum and the Sword* (1946). Geertz offers an interesting analysis of it: "This ethnography from afar starts out trying to expose the workings of Japanese society to make it more accessible, but by the end of the book has succeeded in accentuating its strangeness and has persuaded us that they are a truly odd people" (Geertz 1988, p. 87). Thus, the "great Japanese myth" was created which pictured Japan as a homogeneous patriarchal culture and, according to Geertz, "'the Impossible Object', an enormous something, intricate, and madly busy, that, like an Escher drawing, fails to compute – a challenge not just to our power, but to our powers of comprehension" (Geertz 1998, p. 85). Clearly, the distance to this kind of the Other would seem hard to overcome.

In his research, Rosen asks the question of whether there is a way out of this "epistemological nightmare or crisis of understanding" (Rosen 2000, p. 16). He offers a solution by way of sacrificing one's own perspective and "seeing through of those structures which, by their very nature, tend to resist being seen through" (Rosen 2000, p.16). In other words, it would certainly help in the field of cross-cultural communication to get rid of pre-asserted assumptions and stereotypes and to act without projecting the pre-existed image on the cultural other.

2.1.2 Self-Orientalism

Self-orientalism is a concept indicating practices of reframing and an extension of orientalism. It suggests that Orientalism, in many cases, is not just a Western formation but rather is constructed with the help of the Orient itself. Self-orientalism usually describes a culture "…adopting and absorbing Western hegemony" (Huisman 2011, p. 25) by exploiting orientalist views with the goal of turning the self into the cultural "Other" (Iwabuchi 1994). As Lozano-Mendez points out,

Self-orientalism takes the images supplied by Western orientalism and changes their polarization from negative to positive. The mutual feedback benefits power structures both internationally and within Japan, where the *nihonjinron* – a trend of publications analysing the "particularism" of Japanese people – already promotes conformity to specific models of citizenship (Lozano-Méndez 2010, p. 187).

In the process of self-orientalisation, the drawbacks become assets: "robotic, gregarious and self-emasculated way of life is presented as a considerate, balanced and reliable behaviour" (Lozano-Méndez 2010, p. 188). It is argued by many that in order to create the theory of Japanese identity (*nihonjinron*), Japaneseness has to be imagined by the Other as well as by its own members, though differently (Iwabuchi 1994, p. 51). Thus, Japan's own perception of Japaneseness borrowed and applied the notion of "uniqueness" of the Japanese culture and its ultimate difference from the West.

2.1.3 Techno-Orientalism

Techno-orientalism presents an alternative to the range of exotic stereotypes about Japan, which were popular in Western culture until the second half of the twentieth century. Techno-orientalism emerged with the rise of Japanese economic power, presenting a technological challenge to Europe and the United States. This new techno-version of the Japanese image creates a sort of satirical pastiche from the techniques of cyberpunk and sci-fi literature and represents Japan as a technological superpower. The term techno-orientalism was first used by David Morley and Kevin Robins in 1995: "A new techno-mythology is being spun", where "Japan has become synonymous with the technologies of the future – with screens, networks, cybernetics, robotics, artificial intelligence, simulation" (Morley&Robins 1995, p. 168). As Lozano-Mendez explains, "It refers to a discourse that, from the sixties onward, has promoted an array of stereotypes and deformations about Japan, so that the country has come to epitomize a hyper-technified, dehumanized and materialist society" (Lozano-Méndez 2010, p. 183). Japan was by no means the only country to receive the techno-orientalist treatment. According to Lozano-Mendez, "[i]n the eighties and the nineties techno-orientalist images begun to be projected on other East Asian populations (Taiwan, Singapore, South Korea, and China)" (Lozano-Méndez 2010, p. 183) but Japan was definitely the first in this regard.

Posadas understands techno-orientalism as a phenomenon directly linked to cultural representations of Japan. The researcher sees it as "the production of 'Japan' as aestheticised spectacle, as image ... [and] ... as image commodity" (Posadas 2011, p. 84). O'Donnell supports this opinion by claiming that techno-orientalism is "the representation of contemporary urban Japanese society as technocratic, mechanised, saturated with gadgetry, yet still nostalgically harking back to Western notions of 'mysterious East' and the 'romantic Orient'" (O'Donnell 2015, p. 51). Below I will try to demonstrate how Murakami's and Mitchell's novels engage in this particular type of orientalist polemics.

Techno-orientalism, just as the Saidian approach to orientalism, implies certain cognitive strategies which define how Western people perceive things as "Japanese" – certain pre-existing stereotypes telling what exactly "Japanese" means. Thus, techno-orientalism did not replace "orientalism" but joined into its discourse, freely using all the old stereotypes, prejudices and misconceptions, which go back to the first Jesuit missionaries that visited Japan in 1549. Lozano-Mendez points out that Japan was perceived then as "the world upside down", and "it would seem that they deliberately studied how to differ from everybody" (Lozano-Méndez 2010, p. 185). However, even now, in the age of globalisation and the cross-cultural model of communication, these images did not disappear completely, and Japan is still seen as a mysterious and sometimes dangerous Other. This also reveals, to borrow Wagenaar's words, "a resentful and racist side to this discourse" (Wagenaar 2016, p. 49). Not only is Japan associated with robotics and artificial intelligence, but the Japanese themselves are "dehumanised" by the Western perspective (McLeod 2013). Morley and Robins make it quite clear that techno-orientalism "reinforces the idea of Japan as a cold society, where people themselves are like soulless, efficient machines serving under an authoritarian, bureaucratic culture" (Morley&Robins 1995, p. 169). Through such stereotypes, the West proclaims its own moral and cultural supremacy over Japan.

It is clear that Orientalism has taken many forms and emerged into various types over the years. Though far from being a new concept, it is still widely applicable when a cross-cultural dialogue between East and West is involved. Orientalism, remaining unchanged at its core (trying to reinforce the Western view upon the non-Western cultures), finds new ways of manifesting itself in modern discourses. The case of Japan proves truly unique – apart from the traditional form of Orientalism described by Said (1993), it takes on a techno-orientalist form as well. Moreover, recent studies have shown that there is a new phenomenon, which can be described as "wacky orientalism"[1]. It concentrates

---

[1] So far, I have described the main types of orientalism when it comes to Japan and Japaneseness. Traditional Saidian Orientalism, self-orientalism and techno-orientalism seem to be widely covered in numerous studies. These terms are still in use but it seems that a new version of orientalism has emerged. As Wagenaar notes, "there is a new framework through which Japan is perceived, most notably in popular culture and the media. The West increasingly judges Japan and its people as weird" and this phenomenon can be understood as another model of orientalism: "wacky orientalism" (Wagenaar

on Japan being weird and bizarre in the eyes of the West. All the above demonstrates rather vividly that there is still a lot of work to be done in order to create an environment where it would be possible to see the opposite culture without imposing on it pre-existing stereotypes and misconceptions.

2.2 Techno-Images of Japan in the Works of David Mitchell and Murakami Haruki

> Both internally and externally, images of Japan
> seem destined to be flavoured with fantastic associations
> (Napier 1996, p. 4).

Here I try to trace techno-coloured images of Japan and how exactly they are represented in the works of Murakami and Mitchell. In order to analyse this phenomenon, I use the terms such as techno-orientalism, cyberpunk and remediation. The representation of modern Japan in the works of Mitchell and Murakami appears not only as a deconstruction of stereotypes that have taken root so well in the Western cultural discourse but also as technoculture images (cyberspace, computer games, etc.). Such images seem most appropriate in determining the specific nature of this type of text, which simulates modern

---

2016). The researcher goes on to describe why perceiving Japanese culture as weird can be considered as another type of orientalism and comes to conclusion that "by using this framework of Japan as bizarre, the West confirms what is normal" (Wagenaar, 2016, p.,46). Meaning, of course, that the West is normal and Japan not so much, which brings about a stereotypical attitude that involves seeing Japan as a very different and inferior Other. Wagenaar puts it as follows, "As understood here, orientalism is the act of perceiving cultures as radically different in such a way that it hierarchises them pejoratively in respect to the onlooker's own culture. By framing Japan and its people as weird, the West thus confirms its normalcy" (Wagenaar 2016, p. 47). In a cross-cultural dialogue when facing values and behaviours considerably different from one's own culture it is natural to see strangeness. However, when it comes to Japan it is not limited to a mere strangeness. Popular media articles have long noticed and commented upon this phenomenon: "[i]t's practically a meme in the West: The Japanese are insane. But, you know, loveably insane" (Davis & Yosomono 2012). Thus it is quite clear that although orientalism changed its labels and now targets Japanese "weirdness", it still continues its long-lived tradition to impose stereotypical visions on Japan and dominate it through them, describing it as an inferior Other. Wagenaar claims, "By imagining Japan as weird, the West creates and strengthens the norm of what is normal. Japan does not possess a voice in the creation of this narrative imposed by the West, nor can it really change it" (Wagenaar, 2016, p. 51). Using this perspective, the West speaks for Japan and chooses not to hear the voice of Japan. As Wagenaar concludes, "Thus, Japan is framed as weird, without it being able to challenge that image. By differentiating itself from this strangeness, the West confirms its normalcy" (Wagenaar, 2016, p. 51).

information technology. Such a phenomenon is easier to describe with the term "remediation", which emerged in modern academic fields. Remediation in the culture of the second half of the twentieth century begins to be comprehended and widely applied in modern discourse. The main work in this area is the monograph by David Bolter and Richard Grusin *Remediation: Understanding New Media* (2003), which explores the relationship of literature and art with digital forms of contemporary visual communication. In order to clarify the main points of remediation and its objectives, here I present a brief account of Bolter and Grusins's study given as a book summary:

> Media critics remain captivated by the modernist myth of the new: they assume that digital technologies such as the World Wide Web, virtual reality, and computer graphics must divorce themselves from earlier media for a new set of aesthetic and cultural principles. In this richly illustrated study, Jay David Bolter and Richard Grusin offer a theory of mediation for our digital age that challenges this assumption. They argue that new visual media achieve their cultural significance precisely by paying homage to, rivalling, and refashioning such earlier media as perspective painting, photography, film, and television. They call this process of refashioning "remediation" and they note that earlier media have also refashioned one another: photography remediated painting, film remediated stage production and photography, and television remediated film, vaudeville, and radio (Bolter and Gruzin 2003).

The image of Japan, created by Mitchell and Murakami, imitates, at certain points, and combines different media practices. The literary effect of such remediation is to create an environment in which the reader must process information from various media sources (TV, video games, etc.) to form a certain meaning according to his own understanding of data diversity.

2.2.1 "Japanese" Novels by David Mitchell through the Concepts of Techno-Orientalism and Remediation

Explaining the term remediation in his work "Remediation of Japan in *Nuber9Dream*" (2011), Posadas refers to the process of transfer (or relocation) and implementation of a certain communication/transmission channel into another communication channel. This term emphasises not only the synthesis of the arts and the use of different types of art in a literary work but also the transfer and assimilation of one system of representation of other communication channels in popular culture.

Criticism of "intentional Japaneseness" or focus on orientalism in the works of Mitchell and Murakami is always based on the idea of "authentic" Japan. Modern imagological discourse suggests that "countries and cultures are not pre-existing static entities that exist a priori to their representations" (Posadas 2011, p. 79). Posadas refers to the modern theories which claim that cultures of different countries are only "image commodities that are transnationally produced and cultivated" (Posadas 2011, p. 79). In light of these concepts, it becomes clear that if, for example, the novel of Arthur Holden, *Memoirs of a Geisha*, is more of an orientalist fantasy, Mitchell's works are more of imagological products that, in addition, to a certain extent is "intertextual doppelganger" of the works of Murakami.

The image of Japan in the works of Mitchell and Murakami appears as a quite complex and multi-layered phenomenon that has different levels of representation. Therefore, this industrial and technogenic component of modern Japan's image in the novel *Number9Dream* by Mitchell and *Hard-boiled Wonderland and the End of the World* by Murakami (which I will analyse in the next subchapter) is embodied through cyber poetics and remediation technique. An outstanding feature of these novels is the remediation of the polymedia space: there are computer games and advertising, movies, music, books, and other "mediated cultural practices" in terms of Bolter and Grusin (Bolter and Gruzin 2003).

Posadas understands the image of Japan in Mitchell's works not as a referent for representations but as a space that includes all possible representations (Posadas 2011). Compared with the first Mitchell's novel *Ghostwritten* where the image of Japan is created as a space of so-called "shifting signifiers" (as defined by Posadas, who shares Barthes's view that Japan is "an empire of signs"[2]), in the novel *Number9Dream* Japan loses its status of the geographical phenomenon and becomes a metaconcept compiled from various intertextual remedial and information channels.

Mitchell believes that creating an image of a contemporary Japanese person and Japanese perspective in terms of narrative strategy is the first step towards going beyond Japan's traditional Western orientalist image. As the researcher Nihey Chicako points out in her article "Thinking Outside the Chinese Box", an acceptance of the "Japanese perspective" by the author as a technique is very different from the traditional format in which the West tells about non-West countries within the supposedly objective perspective (Nihei 2009, p. 87). Nihei suggests that Mitchell learned this method from Murakami Haruki (Nihei 2009, p. 87), and in his work, Mitchell also wants, using his own words, "to depict

---

[2] Here I mean Roland Barthes's major work on Japan *Empire of Signs* (1970). With this book, Barthes offers a broad-ranging meditation on the culture, society, art, literature, language, and iconography--in short, both the sign-oriented realities and fantasies--of Japan itself.

Japan as it is". Mitchell stresses that his intention was "to write a bicultural novel, where Japanese perspectives are given an equal weight to European perspectives" (Mitchell 2007b, para. 5). When in one of the interviews with the author, the interviewer Finbow mentions various stereotypes about Japan, such as "geisha", "sarariiman", "Nintend ", "Aum Shinriky ", "manga", Mitchell replies that it is not so bad: "This plurality of lenses is no bad thing: ne view is never enough... We mustn't tell ourselves", "OK, I've got Japanese/UK/Any country culture sussed: I can stop trying to understand it now" (Mitchell 2007b, para. 7). As Nihey observes, the author does not intend to deny the right of existence of the Western view of Japan but tries to point out the importance of a variety of opinions from both outside and inside Japan (Nihei 2009, p. 88).

As for the narrative strategies used to create an image of Japan in such novels as *Number9Dream* by Mitchell and *Hard-Boiled Wonderland and the End of the World* by Murakami, it seems possible to highlight the following features:

1) a clear objective on a techno-oriental image of the country pronounced in subjects and poetics and associated with this attitude of criticism of the theories, which orientalise Japan by means of the Western discourse of Power (all this brings up the problems of transcultural, postcolonial literature and criticism of orientalism);

2) remediation of cyberpunk genre strategies;

3) a specific idea of the big city as a techno-orientalist dystopia.

Thus, Mitchell and Murakami create a techno-orientalism alternative to the exotic stereotype of Japan, which was popular in Western culture until the second half of the twentieth century, using a sort of satirical pastiche from the techniques of cyberpunk literature and representing Japan as a technological country. As Lozano-Mendez explains,

> The term techno-orientalism was coined by David Morley and Kevin Robins in 1995. It refers to a discourse that, from the sixties onward, has promoted an array of stereotypes and deformations about Japan, so that the country has come to epitomize a hyper-technified, dehumanized and materialist society (Lozano-Mendez 2010, p. 183).

The most thorough representation in the literature of techno-orientalism is found in the genre of cyberpunk.

Cyberpunk is generally believed to be a subgenre of science fiction set in the near future and tends to focus on society as "high tech low life". It basically features advanced technological and scientific achievements, such as information technology and cybernetics, juxtaposed with a degree of breakdown or radical change in the social order. Cyberpunk works often describe the conflict between artificial intelligences, hackers, and megacorporations (in the case of

Japan, traditionally known as *zaibatsu*) and tend to be set in the near future rather than in the far-future settings. The genre is often of a post-industrial dystopia but tends to feature extraordinary cultural elements and the use of technology in ways never anticipated by its original inventors. As rightly observed in numerous research works, much of the genre's atmosphere echoes film noir, and written works in the genre often use techniques from detective fiction (Nakamura 2002; Tatsumi 2006).

Such cyberpunk techniques can easily be found in Mitchell's novel *Number9Dream*. For example, there are a lot of open quotations from and mention of such iconic works of cyberpunk as Ridley Scott's film *Blade Runner* and the novel by William Gibson *Neuromancer*. "I have lost track of who is human and who is a replicant on 'Bladerunner'" (Mitchell 2001, p. 296), says Eiji, openly referring to an iconic movie. Allusions to Gibson are more subtle: for instance, the famous opening of Gibson's novel line "The sky above the port was the colour of television, tuned to a dead channel" (Gibson 1984, p. 1) gets transferred in Mitchel's work as "under a sky as stained as a bachelor's underfuton" (Mitchell 2001, p. 14), where both the ironic description of the sky and mentioning of the bio borg taxi refer to Gibson's novel. However, *Number9Dream* cannot be simply reduced just to a straightforward reading as a work of the cyberpunk genre; therefore, it is difficult to agree with the statements of Posadas, who defines the novel that way (Posadas 2011).

The poetics of postmodern work, showing the blurred and ceasing line between reality and unreality of the modern Japanese world with its endless techno-innovations, already existing today or yet to be invented, is subject to the establishment of a monstrous, grotesque ultramodern world where the line between Japanese and non-Japanese is being erased. For example, in *Number9Dream*, Eiji says: "I feel I'm on holiday on another planet, passing myself off as a native alien" (Mitchell 2001, p. 56). Being a Japanese himself, he feels like a foreigner or even an alien dropped off on "planet Japan".

Number9Dream is a novel-grotesque, which mocks in a way the present and future techno-orientalist "japanoid" world that is defined as "the globalist age product" in "The Japanoid Manifesto: Toward a New Poetics of Invisible Culture" (Tatsumi 2002, pp. 2-18). The main idea of the artwork cannot be understood without the ironic subtext and the aggregated and accumulated techniques of literature. Thus, the novel contains not only cyber representations of Tokyo through an endless stream of advertising on billboards, as in the movie *Blade Runner*, and not just representations of Tokyo as an escape of the character into cyberspace through gaming devices. If "reality is the page", then why not a webpage. Within this world, the novel resembles Gibson's *Neuromancer*, which became a classic of the genre. However, *Number9Dream* creates the world of Tokyo and Japan not only as ultra-modern but as phantasmagorical.

It does not seem right to reduce Mitchell's novel to the "doppelganger" of Murakami's works, although the intertextuality of Mitchell's books is related to direct and indirect references to the various works of Murakami (such as *Norwegian Wood*, *Wild Sheep Chase*, *Wind-Up Bird Chronicles*, *Hard-boiled Wonderland and the End of the World*, etc.). The phenomenon of Mitchell's intertextuality and its connection to Murakami's works was analysed in the previous chapter of this research. Mitchell playfully admits it himself in his novel through the words of his character John Lennon who describes his song "Number9Dream" and its relation to The Beatles' song "Norwegian Wood": "'Number9Dream' is a descendant of 'Norwegian Wood'. Both are ghost stories" (Mitchell 2001, p. 398). Although it is the song which Mitchell's' John is talking about, Mitchell himself describes where his novel comes from, meaning Murakami's famous work *Norwegian Wood*.

The creative dialogue of the writers on the problem of representation of Japan and the Japanese national character in modern culture has many similarities in approaches and assessments. The first thing to keep in mind is the rejection of stereotypes of exotic Japan and the representation of Japanese characters in the spirit of "Fuji/cherry blossom/geisha/samurai" or representing Japanese as a harsh militaristic, and fanatic nation. It is also important to understand something that was underlined by Mitchell's character in The *Ghostwritten*: "Phenomena are interconnected regardless of distance" (Mitchell 2007a, p. 266). This interrelatedness of the whole human world, and not the division into an antagonistic confrontation between East and West, is perhaps the central unifying idea of the works of Murakami and Mitchell.

One of the main features of the protagonist strikes from the very first pages of Mitchell's novel *Number9Dream*, defining the narrative strategy that the author uses in his work: Eiji constantly tends to retreat into the world of techno-fantasy, although he often wonders himself as to how "daydreams translate into reality" (Mitchell 2001, p. 4). As it was stated in the epigraph to the novel, which is a quote from the famous novel by contemporary American postmodernist writer Delillo, *Americana*: "It is so much simpler to bury reality than it is to dispose of dreams" (Delillo 1989, p. 334). Most often, Eiji's escape into the digital world of fantasy is accompanied by no signs or signals, which could notify the reader of the transition from the real world to the world of fantasy, and even the character has to ask himself every now and then: "Am I in one of those dreams where the closer you get, the farther away you are?" (Mitchell 2001, p. 24). That is why it is almost impossible to find in the text the line between reality and computer hyperreality. As Posadas underlines, this structure of the text creates a sense of unreliability in the narrative, for the reader never knows for sure if he reads "facts" or dreams (within the artistic world of the novel).

It is easy to notice that Eiji's fantasies are a tribute to popular culture. Scholars emphasise that in Mitchell's writings, it is possible to find out the characteristic feature of the new postmodern culture: a combination of elitism with the mass culture. The first fantasy of Eiji is written in the genre of cyberpunk with a direct reference to it in the text – a quote from the movie *Blade Runner*. For example, the lawyer Eiji is looking for is represented as a cyberpunk "replicant", an android: "A bioborg, dummy! A replicant!" (Mitchell 2001, p. 11). Throughout the narrative, leading features of the genre reveal themselves in different ways. I am going to run through a few of them, giving examples right beside them just to illustrate my point.

1. Cyberspace: widescreen advertising on the streets of Tokyo, virtual games that the old man (Lao Tzu, as Eiji calls him in his thoughts) is playing, arcade games (just as in Gibson's novel *Neuromancer*).

2. Virtual reality: includes all the above, and also Eiji's fantasies that overlap each other starting from the beginning of the novel, when he tries to get to his father's lawyer in one of his fantasies, inventing cunning ways and overcoming many obstacles in his imagination.

3. Artificial intelligence: in the novel, it is presented in the form of a spider from a fairy tale that Eiji reads while hiding from the yakuza in the house of the writer; the spider is called the Queen of plagiarism, and it is described as sitting in the centre of the Internet web and thus is a personalized artificial intelligence of cyberspace.

4. Cyborgs, biorobots: in one of his fantasies, Eiji kills Ms Kano, his father's lawyer, but it turns out she was a cyborg, a replicant, just like in the famous film *Blade Runner*.

5. Urban landscapes described in a post-apocalyptic style: the hero, along with the yakuza, visits different parts of the city, including the night quarters.

6. Large, influential corporations called zaibatsu: in the text, there are none, but a symbol of their powerful clans are the yakuza, and Tower of Panopticon, wherein one of the countless offices Akiko Kano works.

7. Criminal syndicates, mafia: Eiji witnesses yakuza fights and meets *Oyabun*, the yakuza leader of one of the clans.

8. Hackers: in the novel, in a comical way, the author gives a brief description of one of the episodic characters Suga (Eiji works with him at the station), who is a student programmer and whose dream is to steal the holy grail of the Pentagon, which he does eventually.

9. Cybercrime, cyberterrorism: the mentioned hacker's deeds can hardly be called law obedient, especially his farewell gift for Eiji – a CD with a super virus; however, organised cybercrime per se cannot be traced in the novel, just the playful mockery of the genre. Thus, a violation of the law and cybercrime appears only in Suga, who finds out personal information about Miriam.

Thus, most of the characteristics of cyberpunk are somehow embodied in the novel in the form of parody. Posadas defines the main technique that the author uses in the first chapter of the novel as the "technique of surplus signification" (Posadas 2011, p. 82). This technique manifests itself in endless brands and excessive details, which is also one of the attributes of the genre of cyberpunk. It should be noted that Murakami, in his books, sometimes uses very similar strategies, depicting landscapes of urban Tokyo, which I will analyse later. In other words, Tokyo in Mitchell's novel is a place of the disappearance of "real" meanings where "nothing seems real", an abstract city of the future in which it is impossible to trace the origins of anything, a certain simulacrum (in Baudrillard's terms). Eiji, the protagonist of *Number9Dream*, asks himself: "I wonder what Tokyo is for" (Mitchell 2001, pp. 56-57). The speed of life in Tokyo is described by Mitchell in the following way: "Not a single person is standing still. Rivers, snowstorms, traffic, bytes, generations, a thousand faces per minute" (Mitchell 2001, p. 7). Such representation of Tokyo can be related to the words of the famous American pop figure Anthony Bourdain: "Tokyo is like one long film trailer ... the pace getting quicker and quicker, the action more frenzied, leading up to sudden blackness" (Bourdain 2002, p. 136). More clearly, it is manifested in the scene where Eiji sits in a coffee shop, "Jupiter", in the centre of Tokyo and watches the rapid succession of images on the street screens and billboards. This also raises the possibility of the indirect quotation of the model cyberpunk works such as *Blade Runner* by Ridley Scott and *Neuromancer* by William Gibson. In Mitchell's novel, just as in the mentioned iconic works of cyberpunk, Tokyo continually produces images, thus turning itself into an imaginary, nonexistent city. O'Donnell sums up the image of Tokyo in Mitchell's novel as a "conglomeration of buildings, traffic, noise, points of congestion and routes of entrapment and escapes that demarcate its ill-concealed systems of power" (O'Donnell 2015, p. 61). In addition, Mitchell also underlines the anti-humanity of Tokyo, a soulless metropolis, which "turns you into a bank account balance with a carcass in tow" (Mitchell 2001, p. 16); and its unsafety and perils: "If it ain't fire, it's earthquake. If it ain't earthquake, it's bombs. If it ain't bombs, it's floods" (Mitchell 2001, p. 17).

In a way, Tokyo becomes the main character of Mitchell's novel, a kind of "zirconium gothic nightmare", as Eiji defines it, a super monster of automation made out of glass and metal with the stressed technological features, often called or compared to a machine. O'Donnell claims that

> To some degree, the protagonist of this failed and fractured *bildungsroman* is not Eiji Miyake, but the metropolis itself that, beneath its shiny corporate surfaces, chronologies, and organisational systems underlying everything from pizza delivery schedules to gang hierarchies, encrypts the secret of a labyrinthine and chaotic reality (O'Donnell 2015, p. 59)

While it may appear difficult to completely agree about Eiji not being the protagonist of the novel, Tokyo definitely is the focus of the author's attention in the narrative.

Tokyo is also represented as a centre of modernization of Japan, which colonises the country from within. The atmosphere of the techno-landscapes of the city is described by Mitchell in every detail: from the pink love hotels to the luxury meeting rooms where Yakuza sitting at mahogany tables plan their bloody operations. Tokyo workers, "drones", as Eiji calls them, become a kind of faceless background of Tokyo and the novel itself, circling between their work and home. The city lives its own life, conducts its own affairs, constantly producing commodities and destroying the very concept of humanity and thus embodying in itself all the signs of dehumanization. Eiji thinks of it as follows: "Tokyo is a dirty eraser" (Mitchell 2001, p. 164), which underlines the city's skill to eliminate all the feelings and everything alive. O'Donnell points out that

> For Eiji, Tokyo often seems an impossibly convoluted labyrinth of signs, buildings, and crowds that he wanders aimlessly as he pursues the red herrings of his quest. The "barrage of disorienting images" – the sheer randomness of the city – is evident everywhere Eiji goes. (O'Donnell 2015, p. 59)

The image of Japan with its techno-orientalist outlines created by Mitchell is filled with impressive intertextual remediation: computer games, films, Eiji's fantasies in cyberpunk style, billboards, advertisements, etc., as well as references to the works by Murakami Haruki and some other writers – Junichiro Tanizaki, Osamu Dadzai, William Shakespeare, Thornton Wilder, Don DeLillo. This image of Japan contrasts with the rudiments of anachronistic views on decorative Japaneseness: Fuji-Geisha-Samurai, which is also manifested in Mitchell's novel. Posadas claims that this contrast techno-oriental image of Japan is one of the leading features of the new modern aesthetic mode of representation of Japaneseness (Posadas 2011).

Mitchell creates his remediated (if I can apply Bolter's term here) novels fifteen years after the development of the theory of remediation by Bolter: "We call the representation of one medium in another remediation, and we will argue that remediation is a defining characteristic of the new digital media" (Bolter 2003, p. 45). Earlier, there was a similar theory of McLuhan:

> The electric light is pure information. It is a medium without a message, as it were, unless it is used to spell out some verbal ad or name. This fact, characteristic of all media, means that the "content" of any medium is always another medium (McLuhan 1964, pp. 23-24).

The first work by a Japanese author was written in 1979, and Mitchell's first novel was published in 1999, when innovations in technology and communications, which affect our everyday life, radically changed the channels and principles of perception and representation of reality. In Mitchell's novel, *Number9Dream*, the images of modern Japan in general and Tokyo, in particular, appear in the likeness of a supercomputer that threatens to destroy everything human that still exists in this world. Thus, Eiji refers to Tokyo in the following way, taking into consideration its cyberpunk aspects: "These are days when computers humanise, and humans computerize" (Mitchell 2001, p. 115). However, the image of Japan in Mitchell's works cannot be reduced or restricted to this abstract idea, even though the final episode of the novel *Number9Dream* leaves no doubt that the diagnosis that Eiji makes about Tokyo is quite right: a terrible earthquake happens in Tokyo as a response to one of Eiji's fantasies about the destruction of the city. Brightness and accuracy of the media tools the author uses in the novel, including computer games, jazz, movies, Eiji's dreams, fantasies and nightmares and so on, provide the image of Japan with the locally outlined and recognisable traits of a new habitat of humankind.

2.2.2 Dystopian Features of Techno-Images in Murakami's Works

As it was rightly noted by Napier, the twentieth century itself is a world of dystopia (Napier 1996, p. 4). The image of Tokyo in Mitchell's novel largely coincides with the image of a big city in Murakami's works. Both have distinctive features of a dystopian display. Murakami, in his novels, creates a brutal, material, devoid of the cultural and historical colouring dystopian world of ambiguous existence of the lost people. This image of the big city represents the centre of consumer society itself, and the very image of Japan turns out to be a satirical pastiche which is also a product of consumption. Murakami often depicts people who live in Tokyo as lonely and eccentric. In such a way, the writer destroys the stereotype of Japanese corporate unity and morality. His characters, the inhabitants of the big city, are often miserable and somewhat lost people: among them, we can find a man who was nauseous for about forty days (a story "Nausea", 1979), a woman who could not fall asleep for seventeen days (a story "The Sleep", 1992), a girl who, by contrast, could sleep for several months without waking up (a novel *After Dark*, 2007), a man who can communicate with cats (a novel *Kafka on the Shore*, 2002), a mute (character ironically called Cinnamon from the novel *The Wind-Up Bird Chronicle*, 1994-1995), a mysterious girl with dyslexia (a novel *1Q84*, 2013) and many others.

In Mitchell's novels, the Japanese are also depicted as lonely people lost in this huge terrible world, and the author does a good job representing all kinds of characters: yakuza leaders, hostesses from the night clubs, a landlord from the video rental, hairdressers, pizzeria night workers, and even a hacker. The latter character is a kind of embodiment of a cyber city itself, a particular image that defines the created city's features: billboards, constant flow of information, technological world, and modern dystopia.

Napier, in her monumental work *The Fantastic in Modern Japanese Literature: The Subversion of Modernity* (1996), claims that

> In its own way the idea of Japan itself is at the convergence of Utopian and fantastic traditions, a country whose economic success has defamiliarized the very notion of capitalist development by allowing the West to see itself through a glass darkly (Napier 1996, p. 4).

Napier also notes that there is a certain difference between Western and Japanese dystopia: traditional Japanese dystopia is usually less concerned about the loss of personal freedom or will.

> Modern Japan has contained both Utopian and dystopian aspects, not only in the eyes of its citizens, but in the eyes of the West as well. Exotic, even larger than life, Japan seemed in the twentieth century to be constituted in extremes (Napier 1996, p. 179).

We should remember, though, as it has been noted repeatedly, that the very idea of Utopia as it was during the Enlightenment period, the dream of the future, turns out to be a nightmare. Researcher Winter, analysing the genre of Utopia, states that in the twentieth and twenty-first centuries, "The order of things is achieved from the inside out, without any connection to reality, the beautiful symmetry of things becomes in the process a symmetry of evil. The idea of order becomes a terrorism of order" (Winter 1985, p. 102). However, Japanese dystopias are mostly concentrated on the topic of technological nightmares. It is emphasised that the Japanese gladly adopt this aspect (and even to a larger extent than Western writers), pointing out not only the general "failure" of the technology but "the dark interlocking nexus between industry, science, and the military" (Napier 1996, p. 187).

In the works of Murakami, the image of Japan also emerges as cyberspace; Napier defines some of them in the following way: "a fascinating work which problematises the question of both Utopia and dystopia within a high-tech information-driven society" (Napier 1996, p. 187). Most definitely, it can be traced in such novels as *After Dark* and *Hard-boiled Wonderland and The End of the World*. The writer compares the city with a permanently functioning body or artificial intelligence of a supercomputer:

> In our broad sweep, the city looks like a single gigantic creature - or more like a single collective entity created by many intertwining organism. Countless arteries stretch to the ends of its elusive body, circulating a continuous supply of fresh blood cells, sending out new data and collecting the old, sending out new consumables and collecting the old, sending out new contradictions and collecting the old. To the rhythm of its pulsing, all parts of the body flicker and flare up and squirm. Midnight is approaching, and while the peak of activity has passed, the basal metabolism that maintains life continues undiminished, producing the basso continuo of the city's moan, a monotonous sound that neither rises nor falls but is pregnant with foreboding (Murakami 2007, p. 3).

Murakami's image of Japan also includes certain dystopian features. In the works of both Mitchell and Murakami, the crisis of the protagonist is always associated with the changing urban landscape that belies the main character's expectations of the specific presence of something permanent. Consequently, the landscape itself, as well as the character's personality, is to be in continuous fragmentation and deconstruction. It should be noted that the concept of landscape in the works of Murakami was studied by prominent Japanese researcher Karatani (1999), who saw in it an epistemological inversion of consciousness. It is what can be related to the works of Mitchell and Murakami as the image of the urban landscape and perception of it by the protagonist in shaping the image of modern Japan.

The narration in Murakami's novel *Hard-boiled Wonderland and the End of the World* (1985) is divided into two separate narratives that depict two different worlds – "Wonderland", which is an urban dystopia, and "the End of the World", a mythical dystopia masquerading as a Utopian pastoral. Thus, in the narrative of "Wonderland", the image of Japan is manifested as a stereotypical techno-orientalist image of a dystopian world. Events are taking place in Tokyo in the nearest future in which the two media organisations (corporate conglomerate "System" and illegal information mafia "Factory") are waging war for information and power. Generally, all part of the "Wonderland" is a sort of pastiche based on different genres of pop culture. Thus, the old genius scientist turns out to be eccentric and good-natured, which is apparently a reference to the tradition of science fiction of the 1950s. Shadow corporation "System" and its equally shadowy antagonist "Factory" compared with the genre of "paranoid horror" (in Napier's terms), which refers to the works by Kobo Abe and the discourse of beating the system. As for the information wars in high-tech style, it is possible to assume those are a clear intertextual reference to cyberpunk fiction and works by William Gibson, who so brilliantly illustrated "data dance" (and coined the term, too). A witty lone protagonist, on the other hand, points to the tradition of the "hard-boiled detective genre", and the whole narrative structure reminds one of a "well-worked-out" whodunit. Murakami, like Mitchell, builds a literary image of Japan at the crossroads of many traditions of pop culture, hiding behind such a "not serious" form of some serious issues of identity and understanding of Japaneseness.

The leading role in the representation of Tokyo in the novel Murakami belongs to the descriptions of the Tokyo subway, which represents contemporary Japanese fears related to the Sarin attack of 1995. Thus, in the subway of "Wonderland", there are some appalling living creatures, *yamikuro*, who hunt, reside and "hunt" in the dark world of the underground. This image also echoes another Murakami story, "Super-Frog Saves Tokyo", where a huge toad goes to the Tokyo subway in order to exterminate the main threat of Tokyo, embodied in the huge worm. Murakami's Tokyo appears to be a dismal and alienated city, a world based on the principle of mindless consumption of products, from Italian food to media. Technology is out of control and becomes extremely dangerous; it even justifies violence. Furthermore, the union of groups that are supposed to be hostile towards each other– "Systems" and "Factory" – recreates the image of the state, where politicians are in constant and tight collaboration with criminals and where citizens are always oppressed and misinformed. This forms the image of the country, which more or less reflects modern Japan.

Representations of urban life in Murakami's works are a kind of escape into everyday reality (cooking, washing, cleaning, shopping, pools and bars). In Mitchell's novel *Number9Dream*, the image of the postindustrial city is functionally different: it is a background for coming of age. As was stated earlier, in Murakami's urban texts, we fail to find the figure of a parent (or family at all). In Mitchell's works, on the contrary, we can see the image of a protagonist trying to establish family relationships and find some warmth (which can be traced even in its relations with the cat).

Both of the authors depict the situation as the imaginary destruction of the city and its gloomy landscapes. Murakami, in the last episode of his short story "A Slow Boat to China", illustrates this in the following excerpt:

> Our city, these streets, I don't know why it makes me so depressed. That old familiar gloom that befalls the city dweller, regular as due dates, cloudy as mental Jell-O. The dirty facades, the nameless crowds, the unremitting noise, the packed rush-hour trains, the gray skies, the billboards on every square centimeter of available space, the hopes and resignation, irritation and excitement. And everywhere, infinite options, infinite possibilities. An infinity, and at the same time, zero. We try to

scoop it all up in our hands, and what we get is a handful of zero (Murakami, 1993, p. 238).

Another example can be found in this passage as well:

Tokyo – one day, as I ride the Yamanote Loop, all of a sudden this city will start to go. In a flash, the buildings will crumble. And I'll be holding my ticket, watching it all. Over the Tokyo streets will fall my China, like ash, leaching into everything it touches. Slowly, gradually, until nothing remains. No, this isn't a place for me. That is how we will lose our speech, how our dreams will turn to mist. The way our adolescence, so tedious we worried it would last forever, evaporated (Murakami, 1993, p. 238).

Mitchell does it just as well: we can find it in Eiji's fantasy about the flood, which brings destruction to the city and death to Eiji himself. It can also be found in another of Mitchell's novels, *Ghostwritten*, where the protagonist Quasar is willing "to clean" Tokyo and all of Japan. Another of Mitchell's characters character Satoru also thinks about Tokyo with despair:

Twenty million people live and work in Tokyo. It's so big that nobody really knows where it stops. It's long since filled up the plain, and now it's creeping up the mountains to the West and reclaiming land from the bay in the east. The city never stops rewriting itself. In the time one street guide is produced, it's already become out of date. It's a tall city, and a deep one, as well as a spread-out one. Things are always moving below you, and above your head. All these people, flyovers, cars, walkways, subways, offices, tower blocks, power cables, pipes, apartments, it all adds up to a lot of weight. You have to do something to stop yourself caving in, or you just become a piece of flotsam or an ant in a tunnel. In smaller cities people can use the space around them to insulate themselves, to remind themselves of who they are. Not in Tokyo. You just don't have the space, not unless you're a company president, a gangster, a politician or the Emperor. You're pressed against people body to body in the trains, several hands gripping each strap on the metro trains. Apartment windows have no view but other apartment windows (Mitchell 2007a, p. 37).

Such an attitude towards a big city, demonstrated by Murakami's and Mitchell's protagonists, signals the anxiety and depression associated with urban life, which is transformed into the question often asked by the characters: "What am I doing here?" The protagonist in *Ghostwritten* answers this question quite ironically: "Sorting out the meaning of existence" (Mitchell 2007a, p. 48). Mitchell's and Murakami's characters do seem to implement their searches in clearly defined techno-orientalist dystopian decorations.

It is also worth mentioning that both Mitchell and Murakami use numbers and dates as a distinctive feature of their writing, showing the "digitization" of the world and the "self": in Murakami's works, we can find a constant game with dates (mentioning the year of the events without naming the event, such as 1969 – the year of the student movement in Japan), and Mitchell massively plays with the number "nine", starting from the very title of his novel.

2.3 Conclusion

The narrative technique and the semantics of the images created by Mitchell and Murakami demonstrate the obvious link between their works and the techno-orientalist model of the image of Japan. As it was shown above, techno-orientalism is a combination of the depiction of the images of high technology and anachronistic images of exotic Japan. In the novels of Murakami and Mitchell, information networks and spaces are combined with an exotic urban landscape. Depiction of modernity takes place in a slightly fetishized form. The image of Japan acquires unlimited number of images in which the reality of Japan itself is lost. Techno-orientalist poetics of Mitchell's novel is a kind of encyclopaedia on parody and pastiche about cyberpunk, continuous quotation of cross-referential and techno-orientalist images. This technique has much in common with the works of contemporary writers in the East and the West, such as *Neuromancer* by William Gibson, *The Dream Messenger* (*Yumezukai*) by Masahiko Shimada, *Paprika* by Yasutaka Tsutsui and so on.

An important feature in the works of Mitchell is that they are not limited to constant references to Murakami's and Gibson's works. Mitchell also performs certain narrative experiments with mass media culture, which are not separate "excessive" patches and details (teleportation, spaceships, air-taxi, etc.) but the text itself. Both Mitchell and Murakami find a new way of representing futuristic Japan without making it too fantastic and "science fiction", showing it in more realistic ways. In such a combination of realistic and techno-oriental techniques lies the talent of the mentioned writers.

Chapter 3
Representations of Violence as Part of the Image of Japan in the Works of David Mitchell and Murakami Haruki

> Violence is the key to Japan
> (Murakami 1996, p. 60)

3.1 Theoretical Background and Types of Violence

After presenting the analysis of intertextual connections between the works of Murakami Haruki and David Mitchell in Chapter 1 and looking into techno-orientalist images of Japan in the works of the two authors in Chapter 2, I am going to continue to explore the links between the writers and how they represent Japan. In this chapter, I concentrate on a common stereotype of Japanese cruelty and violence manifested and deconstructed in the works of David Mitchell and Murakami Haruki. This stereotype which can be found in the mass culture of the West, is often associated with the ethics of samurai, but it would be a mistake to think that it is limited only to that.

Needless to say, violence in Japan (as well as attitude towards it) has its own history and cannot be equalled to or thought of as the same as violence in Western countries. It is important to keep this in mind while looking into Japanese violence. However, my focus here is not on violence in Japan per se but on how it is depicted in the works of literature, mainly in the novels by Murakami and Mitchell. Thus, here I analyse not the actual phenomenon but rather its literary representation. Nevertheless, in order to do so, I use the theoretical framework created by prominent thinkers in the field of sociology, anthropology and philosophy, such as Walter Benjamin, Slavoj Zizek and Michael Blain. This way, it is possible to understand the cultural logic of violence and its function in society from the standpoint of philosophy, which seems to be helpful in my analysis of the literary works. Therefore, as the theoretical background of this chapter, the following works were used: "Critique of Violence" (1921) (Zur Kritik der Gewalt) by Walter Benjamin; *Violence: Six Sideways Reflections* (2007) by Slavoj Žižek; and *Progressive Violence: Theorizing the War on Terror* (2018) by Michael Blain and Angeline Kearns-Blain.

First, I will address briefly the main points of these works. In his "Critique of Violence" (Zur Kritik der Gewalt), Walter Benjamin observes that violence is to be critiqued on the basis of its relations to law; within the framework of ethical life in the state (sittliche Verhältnisse). He claims that "a cause becomes violent, in the precise sense of the word, when it enters into moral relations" (Benjamin 1921, p. 236). Benjamin is thus interested in the violence present within society and the state.

In *Violence: Six Sideways Reflections* (2007), Slavoj Žižek makes the following distinguishes between the various types of violence:

- the obvious signals of violence, which he calls visible "subjective" violence: acts of crime and terror, civil unrest, and international conflict (violence performed by a clearly identifiable agent).

- "objective" kinds of violence: first, a "symbolic" violence embodied in language and second, a "systemic" violence or the catastrophic consequences of the smooth functioning of the economic and political systems (Zizek 2007, pp. 1-2).

In their collective work, *Progressive Violence: Theorizing the War on Terror* (2018), Michael and Angeline Kearns-Blain study the role of collective violence in the achievement of solidarity. The authors examine the difficulty faced by sociology in theorizing violence and warfare as a result of the discipline's tendency to idealize society in an attempt to legitimize the idea of progressive social change.

The choice of these works is dictated by the timeframe and academic acclaim that those works gained. Benjamin's work is one of the first works on violence in the twentieth century, and its impact is still felt, being referenced in all the subsequent works on violence. Zizek's work was chosen because it is the most resonating research in the field in recent times, providing analysis of the current cultural and sociological processes. Blain's work, to my knowledge, is the latest significant research on violence, and though it is concentrated mostly on American realities, the theoretical aspect of it seems to be applicable to any analysis of violence.

In the abovementioned theoretical works on violence, there is always a focus on and link between violence and society, state, and ideology – something that Murakami calls "The System" in his famous Israel speech (Murakami 2009b). It is important to keep this in mind while analysing Murakami's and Mitchell's works, where there are a lot of manifestations of what Zizek calls visible "subjective" violence, which I will attempt to analyse and classify below. Specifically, I am going to research the following aspects and types of violence, which find their representations in the works of the two authors: exotic representations of violence (the ethics of bushido, samurai and yakuza), criminal violence, violence during historical events (representations of World War II, student movement of the late 60s), domestic violence, and "internal enemies" (terror of "Aum Shinrikyo").

As I show in the following analysis, the most important and widely represented topic regarding violence in the works of the two authors is the topic of religious violence and "inner terror", which refers to the tragic Sarin attack on the Tokyo subway in 1995 and the activities of the religious sect Aum Shinrikyo. I claim that both Murakami and Mitchell explore this theme in depth and have a lot of similarities in their representations. Other images of violence in the works of Japanese and English writers are notably different. Murakami focuses on understanding the historical aspect of the problem, such as violence of the Japanese towards the Chinese during World War II in *The Wind-Up Bird Chronicle* (2010) and *Killing Commendatore* (2018), including the broader context of the attitude of the Japanese to the Chinese in postwar Japan (the cycle of novels *The Rat Series* (2002-2004), the story "Slow Boat to China" (1993) and other novels, including *After Dark* (2007). Murakami also depicts the violent repression of the student movement by the government in 1969 in the novel *Norwegian Wood* (2010), *The Rat Series*, etc. and addresses the problem of the domestic violence and destructive powers of an average person (*After Dark* and *1Q84*).

By contrast, as I prove later, English writer David Mitchell refers to common Western stereotypes associated with samurai ethics. First of all, this kind of ethics is embodied in the "spirit of the Yamato warrior" of the Japanese Army during the Second World War. This might be related to the discourses of Japanese identity and uniqueness, widely known as *nihonjinron*. For instance, these concepts are embodied in the image of Eiji Miyake's grandfather, Subaru Tsukiyama, who was a pilot-kamikaze of a submarine boat-torpedo. Additionally, this ethic is represented in "samurai" traditions of the modern criminal groups of yakuza, which the writer skilfully depicts in his novel *Number9Dream*. Unlike David Mitchell, the Japanese author does not address these clichéd images and does not try to study the "samurai spirit", nor does he ever mention the cherry blossoms as a symbol of Japan.

Before starting a detailed analysis of the representations of violence in the works of the two authors, I would like to begin by clarifying Murakami's views on violence since it was he who claimed that "violence is the key to Japan" (Buruma 1996, p. 60).

3.2 Murakami's Position on Violence

At the ceremony of the Jerusalem Prize in 2009, addressing the issue of violence in his speech, Murakami created a vivid and powerful image of the wall and the egg. He claims that the egg – common people – always breaks down against the wall – The System, but in this battle, the Japanese author is always on the side of the egg.

> "Between a high, solid wall and an egg that breaks against it, I will always stand on the side of the egg". Yes, no matter how right the wall may be and how wrong the egg may be, I will stand with the egg. Someone else will have to decide what is right and what is wrong; perhaps time or history will decide.
>
> What is the meaning of this metaphor? In some cases, it is all too simple and clear. Bombers and tanks and rockets and white phosphorus shells are that high, solid wall. The eggs are the unarmed civilians who are crushed and burned and shot by them. This is one meaning of the metaphor.
>
> Each of us is, more or less, an egg. ... And each of us, to a greater or lesser degree, is confronting a high, solid wall. The wall has a name: It is The System. The System is supposed to protect us, but sometimes it takes on a life of its own, and then it begins to kill us and cause us to kill others – coldly, efficiently, systematically (Murakami 2009b, para. 10)

As we can see from the passage above, Murakami has explained the metaphor "the wall and the egg" not only at the level of a concrete example of the Israeli / Palestine violence but also at the meta-level of individual responsibility and the very origins of any systematic violence, which goes beyond the "visible" phenomena. Murakami says, "We are all human beings, individuals transcending nationality and race and religion, fragile eggs faced with a solid wall called The System" (Murakami 2009b). Therefore, along with interpreting the representation of individual/subjective violence at the religious, socio-political, criminal, and domestic levels, it is necessary to address the representations of Japan as an abstract but at the same time a complex violence system, or as "a systemic violence" in terms of Zizek. As Critchley points out while analysing Zizek's views on ideology and violence,

> Far from existing in some post-ideological world at the end of history where all problems can be diagnosed with neo-liberal economics and self-serving assertions of human rights, ideology completely structures our lived reality. This ideology might be subjectively invisible, but it is objectively real (Critchley 2008, para. 5).

Thus, in his Israeli speech, in such an artistic, metaphorical form, Murakami outlines the range of his creative interests and his position as an author. The writer examines the bloody inheritance that modern Japan has received from the past and relates the evil to the long-standing authoritarian traditions of the Japanese government, responsible for the numerous murders of the Chinese and the sacrifice of millions of Japanese people during World War II, for suppressing student idealism in the late 1960s, for the events occurring in a Tokyo subway in 1995, and for the current boredom and tiredness of the over-saturated Japanese society. Due to all this, the range of ideas in all his works is much wider and deeper. It is never just a problem of an unsuccessful marriage (as in *Wind-Up Bird Chronicle*) or a lost friend (*The Rat Trilogy*) on which the critics sometimes focus the most. The nationalist theory called *nihonjinron* and the tragic events in Japan (especially the gas attack on Tokyo Subway) give the writer a reason to conclude that "violence is the key to Japan" (Buruma 1996, p. 60). In one of his recent interviews for Nagasaki Shinbun, Murakami explains this violence in terms of the darkness of one's heart: "One can't help but feel in the everyday things the signs of violence lurking in the dark world of the bottom of one's heart. One may even feel the horror that such things will emerge from the past"[1] (Murakami 2019, p. 12). Murakami's characters face ugly aspects of the recent history of their country, with cruelty, horrors and lies hidden behind external well-being, and try to historically comprehend what it means to be Japanese in the perception of the modern world.

Murakami, in his works, makes an attempt to identify the internal logic of cruelty and violence in modern society and also ponders the mechanisms of their cultural regulation. Special attention is given to the aspect of the violence associated with the religious sect Aum Shinrikyo, which declared its existence in 1995 with the Sarin tragedy. "Aum" references[2] became part of popular culture in Japan and are one of the common images of modern Japan to the outside world. The fact that this topic is written about by both Japanese and English writers demonstrates the relevance of the study of this phenomenon.

Murakami, in his works *Underground* (1997) and *Underground 2* (or *At the Promised Land*, 1998), which belong to the nonfiction genre, gives detailed portraits and interviews not only of the people who fell victim to a famous

---

[1] Translation is mine. Original quote: 心の底の闇の世界に潜む暴力性のしるしのようなものを、日常的なものごとの中に感じないわけにはいかないのです。過去からそんなものがよみがえってくるような恐ろしさを感じることがあります (Murakami　2019, p. 12)。

[2] Significant in this area are the movies "A" (1998) by Tatsuya Mori, "Where Does Love Go?" ("Ai no Yukue", 2012) by Bunyo Kimura and "Lurking — The Silence of the Cult" ("Senpuku", 2013) by Nobuhiko Hosaka. Furthermore, some popularity gained TV series "Bloody Monday" (2008) and "20th Century Boys" ("Nijusseikishōnen", 1999)

tragedy which happened on March 20 in Tokyo. The author goes as far as to portray the ordinary members of the sect, too. In *Underground*, Murakami explains the necessity of such a move as follows:

> The Japanese media had bombarded us with so many in-depth profiles of the Aum cult perpetrators – the "attackers" – forming such a thick and seductive narrative that the average citizen – the "victim" – was almost an afterthought. "Bystander A" was glimpsed only in passing (Murakami 2010d, p. 7).

> No, what we need, it seems to me, are words coming from another direction, new words for a new narrative. Another narrative to purify this narrative (Murakami 2010d, p. 278).

As Lewis claims, "It is these 'lesser' or peripheral historical narratives that Murakami focuses on, asserting that every story counts, that one story alone could not be representative of the whole country" (Lewis 2013, para. 30). All the above becomes the reason for writing the book and giving some insights into Japanese society.

Ten years later, Murakami returns to this topic and, this time, develops it on a different level in the novel *1Q84* (2013), putting the actions of a mighty sect in a parallel, unreal world, where evil in its global sense is embodied in peculiar mystical creatures, called Little People. It is interesting to note that while speaking about his work during the process of writing it, the author confesses that he intended to create a giant novel that would absorb all the chaos of the world and clearly show the direction of its development:

> What I really want to depict is the good power of the narrative. It is the evil power of the narrative that curses people who are locked inside such closed circles as Aum. This evil power attracts people and leads them the wrong way. What novelists are trying to do is to provide people with a broader meaning and throw them off balance mentally. Novelists try to show what is wrong. I believe in the good power of such narratives, such stories. That is why I want to write a long novel and make the circles of the story larger and work with as many people as possible. To be clear, I have to write a story that can compete with fundamentalism and regionalism (Murakami 2009a para. 30) [3].

---

[3] Translation is mine. Original quote:「僕が本当に描きたいのは、物語の持つ善き力です。オウムのように閉じられた狭いサークルの中で人々を呪縛するのは、物語の悪しき力です。それは人々を引き込み、間違った方向に導いてしまう。小説家がやろうとしているのは、もっと広い意味での物語を人々に提供し、その中で精神的な揺さぶりをかける

Apparently, the "fundamentalism and regionalism" in Murakami are not limited only to religious violence. It is also the image of the sect in general, the leader's figure, and the image of Little People and their strange appearance in "this world". Murakami represents the image of Japan in these novels as the image of the country, which appears to be a repository of violence, and not always noticeable in that way, too, which brings about the notion of Zizekian systematic violence yet again. It was noted that very often Murakami "integrates the private with the public, emphasising that people tend to concern themselves with personal matters before thinking of themselves in the grand, historical scheme of things. Personal events often coincide with historical events, blurring the character's perception of both" (Lewis 2013, para. 33). Such a technique becomes a characteristic feature of Murakami's writing style in which he combines personal and social, individual memory and history.

In the afterword to The *Underground*, which has the title "Blind Nightmare: Where Are We Japanese Going", Murakami notes that the decision to write this documentary was dictated primarily by the fact that the author always wanted to "understand Japan at a deeper level" (Murakami 2001, p. 235):

> A little while after the events, a thought occurred to me. In order to understand the reality of the Tokyo gas attack, no study of the rationale and workings of "them", the people who instigated it, would be enough. Necessary and beneficial though such efforts might be, wasn't there a similar need for a parallel analysis of "us"? Wasn't the real key (or part of a key) to the mystery thrust upon Japan by "them" more likely to be found hidden under "our" territory? (Murakami 2001, p. 235)

Thus, in his "non-fiction" book, the writer joins the anthropological and cultural discourse on Japan and the Japanese outlined by Benedict (1967), Buruma (1996), Posadas (2011), etc. and tries to understand the essence of Japaneseness, to learn more about the national character and society: "I needed to know more about Japan as a society, I had to learn more about the Japanese as a "form of consciousness. Who were we as a people? Where were we going?" (Murakami 2010, p. 235). These questions become the most important in his book, and Murakami, to some extent, tries to find an answer to them, depicting tragedy in which Japanese people participated on both sides – victims and members of the sect responsible for the Sarin attack.

ことです。何が間違いなのかを示すことです。僕はそうした物語の善き力を信じているし、僕が長い小説を書きたいのは物語の環（わ）を大きくし、少しでも多くの人に働きかけたいからです。はっきり言えば、原理主義やリージョナリズムに対抗できるだけの物語を書かなければいけないと思います」(Murakami 2009a, para. 3)

Despite this explicitly stated "Japanese" task the author sets, most of the novels by Murakami are often called "aggressively non-Japanese", and his works are exactly the opposite of the works of such tradition-oriented Japanese writers as Yasunari Kawabata, who sought to convey the "essence of the Japanese consciousness". Murakami's task, however, is also to understand the essence of Japanese life, but in a particular period of the crisis of humanity in the modern world. Despite his famous rejection of "the conventional notion of Japan as not only racially homogenous but also somehow intellectually and emotionally the same from mind to mind, from prefecture to prefecture"[4] (Lewis 2013), Murakami still focuses on such topics as historical memory, and Japanese cultural identity. Murakami's works represent an important milestone in the study of the problem of representing the national image of Japan. The writer, in conformity with modern post-structuralist theories, argues that the essence of the national character is merely an ideological construct, not a real phenomenon.

3.3 Intertextuality of the Religious Violence in David Mitchell's *Ghostwritten*

David Mitchell, in his debut novel *Ghostwritten* (1999), immediately picks up the topic of religious terror, started by Murakami in his non-fictional books. However, unlike the Japanese author, Mitchell does not document it but artistically embodies the topic in the first and last chapters of his *Ghostwritten*, called "Okinawa" and "Underground". These two chapters are intertextually related to the works by Murakami, which are the source and the origin of the mentioned chapters. In addition, it is possible to trace both artistic and ideological parallelism and points of coincidence between the mentioned novel by David Mitchell and the work by Murakami *1Q84*. As an epigraph to his first work, Mitchell uses the quote from the novel by Thornton Wilder, *The Bridge of San Luis Rey*:

> And I, who claim to know so much more, isn't it possible that even I have missed the very spring within the spring? Some say that we shall never know, and that to the gods we are like the flies that the boys kill on a summer's day, and some say, to the contrary, that the very sparrows do not lose a feather that has not been brushed away by the finger of God (Wilder 1961, p. 9).

---

[4] Later, Murakami changes his mind, saying in a 1996 New Yorker profile written by Ian Buruma that "Japan is a mono-racial country. There is this feeling of togetherness, of sharing a landscape, or the imperial system, or, indeed, the love of listening to insects. This can be a dangerous, irrational force, but I feel part of it. I used to hate it, but now I want to find out what is important to me about Japan". (Buruma 1996, p. 60)

It is known that in his novel, Wilder explores how people with different fates and world perceptions find themselves in one place at one time to accept their mutual outcome, which is death. Similarly, Murakami builds his non-fiction work *Underground*, focusing primarily on the role of chance (as all these people were at the same time on the same train), the personal life and thoughts of the participants of the event, as well as how the tragedy affected their further fate. As a result, Murakami creates a perfect literary space where he can consider what it means to be a Japanese person who faces a tragedy like a gas attack.

David Mitchell, in the chapter "Okinawa" in the novel *Ghostwritten*, relies greatly on the second non-fiction Murakami's book *Underground II*, which contains the testimonies of the sect members who committed acts of terrorism in the Tokyo subway. Significantly, this topic becomes central in the first and last episodes of Mitchell's work, making up the frame composition of the novel.

The main character of Mitchell's novel *Ghostwritten*, in the first and last episodes, is the one who lets out gas in Tokyo subway and flees from Tokyo to Okinawa, hiding from justice. The narrator, nicknamed Quasar, is a member of the religious cult. He believes in the power of the Leader and in the righteousness of the committed act, the need to clean Tokyo and Japan from the "dirt". He sees the "distortion" of Japan and its increasing similarity to the West, especially America: "The same shops as anywhere else ... Burger King, Benetton, Nike ... High streets are becoming the same all over the world, I suppose" (Mitchell 2008, p. 211).

The ideas of dirt, of the collapse of Japan, and of a unique Japanese identity under the onslaught of globalization manifest themselves in the hero's thoughts about the everyday life of distant islands:

> Nobody admits it, but the islands are dying now. The young people are moving to the mainland. Without subsidies and price-fixing the agriculture would collapse. When the mainland peaceniks get the American military rapists off the islands the economy will slow, splutter and expire. The fish are all being fished out by factory trawlers. Tracks lead nowhere. Building projects have been started, but end in patches of concrete, piles of gravel and tall, thorny weed (Mitchell 2008, p. 27).

These images of decline are determined by the desire of the hero to clear his own country and the world in general. Such ideas of purifying the world directly point to the founder of the Aum Shinrikyo sect, Shoko Asahara, who is well-known for justifying evil in order to clean this world from a greater evil.

Significantly, this idea of purifying Japan, initiated by Quasar in the first chapter of his first novel Mitchell, develops in the author's next work, *Number9Dream*. On a rainy day, Eiji Miyake dreams about the symbolic flooding of Tokyo and its cleansing. At the end of the novel, Eiji, while on Yakushima island, finds out that a terrible earthquake occurred in Tokyo.

On another occasion, Quasar thinking of the fate of Japan, notes:

> As I left that memorial to nobility a coachload of tourists arrived. ... It would have appeased the souls of the young soldiers who had died for their beliefs decades ago, as I had been ready to do only seventy-two hours ago. They were betrayed by the puppet governments that despoiled our land after the war. As have we all been betrayed by a society evolving into markets for Disney and McDonald's. All that sacrifice, to build what? To build an unsinkable aircraft carrier for the United States (Mitchell 2008, p. 7).

It should be noted that the sarcastic paraphrase – Japan as "an unsinkable aircraft carrier for the United States" as put by Mitchell, while being a direct reference to Prime Minister Nakasone's remark in the context of Japan's security treaty with the U.S. at the time of President Reagan, may intertextually refer to the famous novel *Japan Sinks* (『日本沈没』, 1974) by another Japanese writer Sakyo Komatsu, which also depicts, in no uncertain terms, the threat of destruction Japan. Such a view of the country's future originates in the genre of "Atomic bomb literature (原爆文学 Genbaku bungaku)" and then develops in the works of Abe Kobo, Komatsu Sakyo, Oe Kendzaburo. Murakami Haruki, as a modern Japanese writer, takes on all of these influences and continues the tradition in its original way.

David Mitchell subsequently picks up these topics, too. Quasar's thoughts about cleansing Japan and his sympathy towards Japanese soldiers who died during the Second World War may be well correlated with the considerations of Eiji Miyake in the novel *Number9Dream*. He is contemplating whether modern Japan is the same country the Japanese soldiers were dying for during the Second World War, including his grandfather Subaru Tsukiyama. He asks what his grandfather would think of modern Japan: "Was it worth dying for? ... Maybe it is a mercy he cannot see the Japan that was chosen" (Mitchell 2001, p. 310).

When reading his grandfather's diaries, Eiji begins to understand the absurdity of the sacrifices made during that tragic time. Significant are Eiji's ideas about himself as a Japanese, a product of modern Japan: "A weird thought, that – I am not made by me, or my parents, but by the Japan that did come into being" (Mitchell, 2001, p. 310).

These words are consonant with Quasar's thoughts, who is a member of the sect and who, moreover, took part in mass murder. He, like Eiji from *Number9Dream*, as well as Satoru from the "Tokyo" chapter of *Ghostwritten*, is a product of modern Japan, an equally important part of the Japanese national and international image and its representation of it.

In Okinawa, Quazar keeps track of the news and sees how all members of the sect are arrested and how they betray each other, giving up the names of the participants, including Quazar himself. However, he has yet to lose trust in the extraordinary capabilities of his mentor yet, and even, as he is sure, "receives messages" from the leader of the sect – through the movements of a spider, through barking of a dog, through the noise of the waves. Eventually, it becomes obvious, though, that something gradually changes in him, especially when he has these memories, or rather recurrent flashbacks, about a little girl in a woolly hat and her sincere smile addressed to him in the death carriage just a few moments before the accident. The character, clearly, has come to doubt the correctness of what he has done: "She knew what I was going to do. And she asked me not to" (Mitchell 2008, p. 25).

3.4 Comparative Analysis of the Representations of Religious Violence

From the previous analysis detailed in Subchapters 3.2 and 3.3, it is clear that in the works by Murakami Haruki and David Mitchell, there are unexpected dimensions of modern Japanese life, one of the manifestations of which is the image of "Japanese terror" "internal enemy" embodied in the activities of the religious group "Aum Shinrikyo", tragically famous for the organising of the sarin attack in Tokyo subway in1995. This topic occupies a separate and important place in the works of the Japanese and English writers. Thus, immediately after the tragedy, two Murakami books appeared: *Underground* (『アンダーグラウンド』, 1997) and *Underground II* (『約束された場所で』, 1998), in which the author makes an attempt to understand the phenomenon of Aum and provide an adequate response to its affiliation to the modern Japanese context. After that, for a while, the writer leaves this topic and does not mention it in his works, although there are some or other dark references to subways and undergrounds in his novels and short stories. However, Murakami explicitly returns to this topic in his multi-volume novel *1Q84* (2013), which indicates the importance of the problem and highlights some unresolved issues associated with it.

Characteristically, David Mitchell begins his creative career contemplating this same problem, masterfully addressing it in his first novel *Ghostwritten* (1999). In doing so, he undoubtedly follows the Japanese author. The English writer picks up and peculiarly develops Murakami's theme of violence as an essential component of understanding Japan's image, especially seen from the outside. This problem is at the centre of this chapter, and it is the one that is common to both writers. However, we note that the problem of Japanese violence is not limited to the image of religious terror and the Sarin tragedy.

In Murakami's works, the image of terrorists as well as ordinary members of the sect, is also ambiguous. The psychological detail in the image of the physician Hayashi, one of the terrorists, conveys it quite clearly. Going into the car and seeing women and children there, he doubts whether he is doing the right thing and therefore releases gas after a certain time, leaving one of the bags with the gas untouched:

> Glancing at a woman and child in the car, Hayashi wavered slightly. "If I unleash the sarin here and now", he thought, "the woman opposite me is dead for sure. Unless she gets off somewhere". But he'd come this far; there was no going back. ... in the end, only one of the two bags was found to have been punctured; the other was untouched (Murakami 2010d, p. 11).

Murakami writes his journalistic investigation in a detached, unbiased style of reporting; meanwhile, Mitchell's novel is a living horror, fear and despair, and later on, a sense of guilt brought out by the impossibility of correcting what was done.

The image of the sect, its subdivisions, ministries, and the leader, presented in the works of Mitchell through the blurred perception of the delusional protagonist, repeats in its structure some of the documentary images created by Murakami. However, not only does Mitchell replicate what has already been depicted, but he also ironically reconsiders the essence of the sect, revealing new meanings and the causes of the "Japanese violence" in the context of bitter reflections on the phenomenon of "Aum" as a component of modern stereotype about the Japanese. From the first word about alpha and gamma rays mentioned by Quasar, it is clear that the Leader in Mitchell's work is a crook, although his religion, as well as the ideas of the real Asahara, the founder of Aum, is spread throughout the world as seen from the following chapters of Mitchell's novel. In Murakami`s works *Underground* and *Underground II*, this exact image starts to be created in the eyes of the Japanese.

The figure of the Leader in Murakami's novel *1Q84* is ambiguous; he is the bearer of "secret knowledge and enormous pain"; he is the one who hears "the Voice". His suffering is so strong that he himself wants to die. And even the assassin girl who was sent to kill him and who knows well about all his crimes and atrocities hesitates to execute him as planned until he himself asks her to do so. Murakami depicts how a person becomes a channel of something terrible without knowing how it happened. In this, we also see some sort of connection with Mitchell's protagonist, whom the author tries not to blame, but understand. In such a non-accusatory and morally indefinable picture of the situation, the characteristic feature of postmodern culture establishing the relativity of value can be found. The debate that broke out concerning the postmodernist axiology "Can Postmodernism Condemn Terrorism?" (Fish 2002) is precisely this.

In the image of a leader of the sect in Murakami's novel appear the thoughts of the writer about the state of modern Japan. Murakami, in his work, speaks of himself as the organizer of the book and the interviewer:

> We will get nowhere as long as the Japanese continue to disown the Aum "phenomenon" as something completely other, an alien presence viewed through binoculars on the far shore. Unpleasant though the prospect might seem, it is important that we incorporate "them", to some extent, within that construct called "us", or at least within Japanese society. Certainly, that is how the event was viewed from abroad (Murakami 2010d, p. 227).

Consequently, Murakami accepts the sarin tragedy as a Japanese phenomenon, tracing the causes of its occurrence to the deep-seated problem of contemporary Japanese society, and tries to look at the Japanese from the outside as well. This confirms the opinion that Murakami is probably the first Japanese writer who, in his work, made an attempt to view Japan through the eyes of a Western man, creating a kind of multidimensional image of Japan, combining both inner and outer perspectives. Murakami admits it openly in the interview with Jay McInerney, where he claims that he moved to America precisely because of the possibility of "write about Japanese society from the outside". Murakami believes that such an attitude defines his "identity as a writer" (McInerney 1992, para. 25).

In the phenomenon of Aum Shinrikyo, Murakami sees a distorted image of Japan and Japanese society – an image that none of the Japanese at the end of the twentieth century could predict. At the time of the attack, the citizens of the country found it hard to believe that such a terrible thing could really occur in Japan, commonly believed both from inside and outside to be a perfectly safe place. Terrorism, according to the common Japanese opinion, is inherent to Western societies, not Japanese. The author, on the other hand, calls the Japanese terrorists and sectarians "*the mirror of us*" (Japanese people) and notes that

> ...a mirror image is always darker and distorted. ... Which is why we avoid looking directly at the image, why, consciously or not, we keep eliminating these dark elements from the face we want to see. These subconscious shadows are an "underground" that we carry around within us, and the bitter aftertaste that continues to plague us long after the Tokyo gas attack comes seeping out from below (Murakami 2010d, p. 229).

The symbolic name of the work, *Underground,* becomes clear in its meaning and significance and is duplicated later on as the name of the last episode of Mitchell's novel, both as the subway and the secret place of the subconscious belonging to a person or even a whole nation. It is worth noting that famous American postmodernist writer Don Delillo implies the same conceptual word game in the title of his well-known novel *Underworld* (1997). Significantly, Mitchell repeatedly references the work of Delillo and even uses the quotation from the novel *Americana* (1971) as an epigraph to his novel *Number9Dream:* "It is so much simpler to bury reality than it is to dispose of dreams" (Delillo 1989, p. 334).

Taking into account such a double perspective (Japan in the eyes of the West and the Japanese themselves)[5], Mitchell also creates a meta-dimension of Japan. The English author, in his hetero-dimensional perspective, adds an auto image projection, introducing the Japanese character and not a foreigner. Mitchell refuses the prospect of "foreign (Western) eyes", creating the image of the country allegedly from the inside, portraying the attitude of the Japanese character without distance. Duplicating the sentiments of surprise about this phenomenon in Japan, which was depicted in Murakami's works (refusal to recognise "us" in "them"), Mitchell portrays "ordinary Japanese" who, after watching the news about the tragedy of the Sarin attack, notes with horror:

> Can't they see that the real atrocity is the modern world's systematic slaughter of man's oneness with his anima? The act of the Fellowship was merely one counterattack against the true monster of our age (Mitchell 2008, p. 10).

These lines show the distrust of the Japanese man and his rejection of the phenomenon as a component of the image of modern Japan, the refusal to see himself from this angle, the refusal to include "them" in the image of "us, the Japanese" which coincides completely with the speculation of Murakami about modern Japanese and Sarin tragedy in the above-mentioned works. Thus, Quasar understands that the cruelty of the sect is a product of the cruelty of the modern world and modern Japan. He recollects his childhood, full of restrictions and bullying at school; and the fact that he becomes a member of a religious group means only that the protagonist sees in it a kind of social protest: "All my life, they had measured every last millimetre of failure and success, and here I was snapping their rule across my knee" (Mitchell 2008, p.

---

[5] Japanese writer Murakami tries to look at Japan from the Western perspective and proves in his writing that Aum is also part of Japan. English writer Mitchell writes from the point of view of a Japanese terrorist and considers the phenomenon from the inside, particularly from the Japanese perspective. His character graciously relates himself to the Japanese nation, he even considers himself a benefactor of Japan – the saviour, purifier. Writers of different nationalities and cultural background seem to be moving toward each other, creating a similar image of Japan with different methods.

10). The village teacher reasonably and soberly analyses the reasons for joining the sect, the episodic character in the chapter "Okinawa" of the novel *Ghostwritten*:

> Maybe there are many answers. Some get a kick out of self-abasement and servitude. Some are afraid or lonely. Some crave the camaraderie of the persecuted. Some want to be big fish in a small pond. Some want magic. Some want revenge on teachers and parents who promised success would deliver all. They need shinier myths that will never be soiled by becoming true. The handing over of one's will is a small price to pay, for the believers. They aren't going to need a will in their New Earth (Mitchell 2008, p. 23).

With these disasters, Mitchell also connects to the world's humanitarian crisis. The character is unable to accept the cruelty and strict regulation of the social system of his country, and this is enough for him to start killing in order to save mankind from its sins. The same substitution of values and the evolution of the goals we can find among sectarians, which researchers write about while studying the phenomenon of Aum: from saving the world from complete destruction[6]. This opinion seems quite correct because, as pointed out by the researchers of religious terrorism, such as Ian Ryder, such a movement puts the centre of forcible subjugation of the individual's will to a religious statute; the interpretation of the same statute is recognised only in the version of the inspiration of the terrorist organisation. The possibility not of thinking independently but of conveying these powers of one's thoughts to the leader seemed attractive to ordinary members of the group. This complex problem is covered by Mitchell in his novel, especially in the conversation between Quasar and a village teacher, which was given above.

Analysing the reasons why ordinary people joined the sect (and not only ordinary – among the elite of the group, there were highly qualified doctors, lawyers, and teachers, which gives rise to certain doubts as to who can be considered a "typical follower" of Aum Shinrikyo), Murakami concludes that they did not find their place in the modern highly regulated Japanese society. Mitchell captures this idea in his novel, using the same images: "We all have an inner self ... This inner self is our own responsibility" (Mitchell 2008, p. 22). The Japanese, who decided to go to the sect, delegated their "inner-selves" to the leader and, in such a way, ceased to control themselves, thus freed from responsibility, which led to the tragedy:

---

[6] In the fundamental work by Ian Reader, *Religious Violence in Contemporary Japan: The Case of Aum Shinrikyo* (2000), the whole chapter entitled "Losing the Struggle – From World Salvation to World Destruction" is devoted to the process described.

I fear that many of the young men and women in the Fellowship handed this inner responsibility to their Guru, to do with as he pleased. And that (…) is what he did with it (Mitchell 2008, p. 22).

In these words, we can see a clear hint to the corresponding lines from the afterword to *The Underground* by Murakami, who resolves the question of responsibility for one's actions and intentions and warns against giving it to someone else: "Are your dreams really your own dreams? Might not they be someone else's visions that could sooner or later turn into nightmares?" (Murakami 2010d, p. 223).

Thus, the complex image of the contemporary Japanese people, frightened by the prospect of staying in a world of strict regulation, and discouraged by the necessity to make their own everyday decisions, is artistically embodied in the lines above. It is the image of the Japanese people who chose to see someone else's dreams to make their existence easier but instead found themselves in "someone else's nightmare" of forced murders and terrorism.

In the last episode of Mitchell's novel *Ghostwritten*, Quasar, in an attempt to jump out of the "death car", sees in the advertisements and posters on the walls around him the events that the writer has already depicted in previous chapters of the novel. This author's approach is intended not so much to combine all of the narratives (most of which appear to have apocalyptic motifs – as a hint to the program of the sect, the expectations of the end of the world and the attempts to bring it closer), but, rather, to write them into the "Japanese" part of the novel, a hint that is repeated and further developed in all the other chapters, replaying the problems set forth at the beginning. Their acute embodiment in the fantastic episodes of the novel is a metaphorical representation of the Japanese tragedy that appears in the novel as a tragedy of humanity.

The works of Murakami and Mitchell are connected not only on a thematic level but also on the level of using concrete images and details. One of the crosscutting symbolic codes that Murakami repeatedly uses in his works is an image of the zoo, a parabolic image that is embodied in world literature in various allegoric ways like *Animal Farm* (1945) by George Orwell, *The Book of Imaginary Beings* (1957) by Jorge Luis Borges, etc. The Japanese author implies it as a part of the image of Japan in his stories "Elephant Vanishes", "A Good Day for a Kangaroo", etc. The most significance this image acquired in Murakami's large-scale novel *The Wind-Up Bird Chronicle*. Incidentally, Mitchell's novel *Ghostwritten* character named Quasar notes: "What a sick zoo the world has become!" (Mitchell, 2008, p. 21), where "the world" stands primarily for Japan. Another character in a novel from another chapter episode, a female Irish physicist Mo, observes how the secret technology developed by her is used for militaristic purposes and exclaims: "My, it's a sick zoo we've turned the world into" (Mitchell 2008, p. 316). Thus, these words that repeat Quasar's thoughts on Japan hold the insertion of Japan in the global context of the crisis of humanity. When Mo leaves the base of the Light Box, she "empties zoos of my most virulent viruses on the disks I'd leave behind" (Mitchell 2008, p. 327). The motive connection to the works of Murakami can be traced to the very concept of "destroying the zoo". The Irish scientist creates a Zookeeper – a computer that monitors that humanity does not destroy itself, and this machine is supposed to be more humane than the people themselves. By contrast, in Murakami's *The Wind-Up Bird Chronicle*, we can find the tragic scenes of the extermination of the (metaphorical) zoo in China by Japanese soldiers while leaving the continent.

Such a resemblance of image usage in the works of Mitchell and Murakami is manifested in intertextuality through deliberate codification and citation in the process of creating the image of modern Japan. However, in his imagological experiment, Mitchell does not limit his creative task to a mere usage of intertextual techniques and simultaneous rethinking of the subjects and images of the Japanese writer. Thus, the image of Quasar is created taking into account the achievements of the wide spectrum of world literature. The blind faith of the protagonist may cause an ironic smile, but the tragedy to which the character was led by this belief is truly frightening. Quasar does not want to admit it to himself, but the fact is that he himself is afraid of what he has committed. He is tormented by nightmares, and he constantly remembers the little girl from the train:

> The baby in the woolly cap, strapped to her mother's back, opened her eyes. They were my eyes. A disembodied voice was singing a chorus over and over again. And reflected in my eyes was her face. She knew what I was going to do. And she asked me not to (Mitchell 2008, p. 25).

Furthermore, he starts to feel unusual sensations in his palms: they pinprick ("Pinpricking in the palm of my hands" (Mitchell 2008, p. 3), as he thinks to himself). It seems to him that they are covered with spots: "My palms have become blotchy. I clean myself eight or nine times a day, but something is wrong with my skin" (Mitchell 2008, p. 25). Intertextual links with Shakespeare's *Macbeth* manifests themselves clearly[7]. At the end of the first chapter episode,

---

[7] The famous tragedy about a Scottish general who becomes a king of Scottland by way of comittimg numerous murderes, urged by his wife. The motif of hands appear in the play when Lady Macbeth is taken into the realm of madness by her increasing feeling of guilt: she tries to wash off imaginary bloodstains from her hands, all the while speaking of the terrible things she knows she pressed her husband to do.

Quasar feels that his "fingernails become loose" (Mitchell 2008, p. 25). This Shakespearian image is also used by Murakami in his novel *1Q84*, where he develops the themes related to the crisis of humanity, which he started to write about in his earlier works *Underground* and *Underground II*. The Japanese writer goes as far as to directly quote *Macbeth*, proclaiming the approach of the unknown evil embodied in LittlePeople, whose voice the sect leader can hear. The quote is the phrase of one of the three witches who feels the approach of the murderer, Macbeth, when her fingers itch: "By the pricking of my thumbs, Something wicked this way comes" (Shakespeare 2000, p. 55). Such unintentional thematic and stylistic connections with the shared source – Shakespeare – in the work of Japanese and English writers testify to their common concern for the fate of the world in general and Japan in particular.

3.5 Individual and Domestic Violence in Murakami's Works

Representation of the violence of Japanese society in the works of Mitchell and Murakami is not limited to the descriptions and questioning of religious terror. In Murakami's works, the theme of wartime atrocities of the Japanese on the continent acquires certain attention, while Mitchell does not explore this topic though he depicts wartime Japan in his *Number9Dream*. Furthermore, the problem of domestic violence, or, more widely, the violence of the modern "ordinary Japanese", is represented in Murakami's works *Kafka on the Shore* (2002), *After Dark* (2007) and *1Q84* (2013).

Describing his 2002 novel *Kafka on the Shore*, Murakami says, "I planned to write about a fifteen-year-old boy who runs away from his sinister father and sets off on a journey in search of his mother" (Murakami n.d., para. 2). Here the figure of the father is described as "sinister" since his secret "hobby" is to kill violently stray cats: "I'm the one who cut off all those cats... I'm collecting them" (Murakami 2006b, p. 129) The father's soul is so dark that Kafka decides to become a homeless runaway instead of living with him: "But I have to get out of here. ... No two ways around it" (Murakami 2006b, p. 4).

In *After Dark* (2007), individual violence is embodied in the descriptions of the "bloody" adventures of an ordinary office worker (*sarariman*), who does his best at work and is an exemplary family man but he beats a half-dead Chinese prostitute. Here is the description of the hotel room after he left:

"Out, damned spot! out, I say!--One: two: why, then, 'tis time to do't.--Hell is murky!" (Shakespeare 2000, p. 74) "What, will these hands ne'er be clean?" (Shakespeare 2000, p. 74) "Here's the smell of the blood still: all the perfumes of Arabia will not sweeten this little hand" (Shakespeare 2000, p. 74).

> The room is windowless and stuffy and all but filled with the oversize bed and TV. Crouching on the floor in one corner is a naked woman in a bath towel. She hides her face in her hands and cries soundlessly. Bloodsoaked towels lie on the floor. The bedsheets are also bloody. A floor lamp lies where it was knocked down. On the table is a half-empty bottle of beer and one glass. The TV is on and tuned to a comedy show. The audience laughs (Murakami 2007, p. 36).

By creating such an image, Murakami shows the dark side of the human soul and places in the Japanese setting, and it becomes a part of his representation of modern Japan.

1Q84 (2013) is another example of the representations of individual/domestic violence. The main female character Aomame is hired by an elderly rich woman who is known by the name "Dowager" to assassinate men who violently abuse their wives. Characteristically, in the novel, most of these exemplary family men occupy high positions in Japanese society. The descriptions of violence are very vivid. For example, sending Aomame on a "mission", the dowager shows her photographs of the abused woman:

> From an envelope lying on the table Aomame took seven Polaroid photographs and set them in a row, like unlucky tarot cards, beside the fine celadon teapot. They were close-up shots of a young woman's body: her back, breasts, buttocks, thighs, even the soles of her feet. Only her face was missing. Each body part bore marks of violence in the form of lurid welts, raised, almost certainly, by a belt (Murakami 2013, p. 95).

Murakami shows that violence gives life to more violence since both the dowager and Aomame do not have a moral problem with killing the abusers and justifying the reasons for doing so.

The topic of individual and domestic violence is vividly present and well-developed in Murakami's works and calls for an in-depth study. However, for the purposes of this research, I introduce it briefly as part of the wider discourse on violence in Murakami's novels. That includes depictions of the historical violence in the works of Murakami and Mitchell, which I will analyse in the following subchapters.

3.6 Historical Violence in Murakami's Representations of Wartime Japan

Historical violence in the works of Murakami mainly manifests itself in his interpretations of WWII and the role of Japan in it. As I try to show in this subchapter, Murakami focuses on the all-penetrating ideology of the state and contrasts it by recounting the personal stories and experiences of ordinary Japanese people. Such a dichotomy easily fits into the framework of the famous postmodern philosophy of the "incredulity towards grand metanarrative" developed and popularised by the French thinker François Lyotard in his monumental work *The Postmodern Condition: A Report on Knowledge* (1979). By way of presenting personal – "small" – narratives, Murakami deconstructs the existing ideological notions on what Japan is and should be, depicting – or rather recreating – a new image of Japan. Such interest in "small" narratives and individual memories and histories correspond with Murakami's position proclaimed in his Israeli speech: "Between a high, solid wall and an egg that breaks against it, I will always stand on the side of the egg" (Murakami 2009b, para. 10). Representations of Japan as a metaphorical struggle between "the wall" and "the egg" is particularly clear in Murakami's war narratives, where the image of the country is split between the ordinary Japanese, both soldiers and civilians and the authoritative militaristic state, which leads the country to the defeat and economic collapse. In this subchapter, I will address this opposition, how it is worded in the writer's novels and what complications it brings about in the context of Japanese image-making.

Representations of wartime Japan, both in terms of the lives of the civilians during the war and the activities of the Japanese army on the continent, take place in quite a few novels of Murakami. Among them particularly worth noting are *A Wild Sheep Chase* (2002), *The Wind-Up Bird Chronicle* (2010), *Kafka on the Shore* (2006), and *Killing Commendatore* (2018). Here I offer a brief analysis of these four novels with a strong focus on *The Wind-Up Bird Chronicle* as it is often considered a pretext of Mitchell's *Number9Dream* (Lesser 2014, p. 66; Mitchell 2009, para.7) and, therefore, greatly influenced Mitchell's representations of wartime Japan, which I describe in the next subchapter.

Murakami's prose is a complex phenomenon well in line with the postmodern literary theories of multiple layers of narration, interlocking narratives and unreliable narrators, so it is no surprise that all his representations of war memory (and subsequently of wartime Japan) appear in his books as parallel narratives, often having nothing to do with the main plot. Thus, the war-related episodes in *A Wild Sheep Chase* (2002) are shown through a [non-existing] book, *An Authoritative History of Junitaki Township*, which the protagonist is reading on a train on his way to Hokkaido. In *The Wind-Up Bird Chronicle* (2010), Murakami depicts war through the respective oral narratives of Lieutenant Mamiya and Nutmeg as well as through letters. In *Kafka on the Shore* (2002), it is war documents and letters to the psychiatrist that bring about the wartime image of Japan. And finally, in *Killing Commendatore* (2018), the war stories are again conveyed orally as rumours and memories, often retold by a person who did not participate in the described events. Except for the war documents, which Murakami unambiguously draws as certainly incomplete if not totally false and hence unreliable (in contrast to the personal account of the same events conveyed to a doctor in personal letters), all war-related narratives are personal, even in the book on Junitaki history, since they focus on the individual experiences and present opinions of the citizens of Junitaki. Murakami's writing strategy is clear; the author prefers to deal with small personal stories as a counter-narrative to the ruling ideology.

It has been noted that Murakami "generally avoided very strong political comment in his works until *The Wind-Up Bird Chronicle*, and since then critics have lauded him for being much more 'engaged' and 'committed' to Japan and its political state" (Sellers 2017, p. 4). As it is clear from the following quote from *1Q84*, Murakami seems to have a problem with the historical narratives constructed by the government in the post-war period:

> Robbing people of their actual history is the same as robbing them of part of themselves...Our memory is made up of our individual memories and our collective memories. ... [a]nd history is our collective memory. If our collective memory is taken from us – is rewritten – we lose the ability to sustain our true selves (Murakami 2013, p. 322).

Expressing his scepticism toward altering certain aspects of Japanese history, Murakami raises the question of identity and the role of collective and individual memory in forming it. The problems of identity and memory in the context of contemporary understanding of Japan's war memory are directly linked to the image of Japan, created and recreated through these elements in the writer's books.

The issue of war memory in Japan is rather a complex one. As was pointed out, a certain controversy exists regarding cultural amnesia towards war events (Orr 2001; Seraphim 2006; Sellers 2017). Murakami, in his work, addresses this problem by depicting violent practices in wartime Japan. Strecher provides the following characterisation of Murakami's anti-war literary statements:

> [Murakami's] work offers an opportunity to revaluate the hypocrisy of a national history that annually commemorates the atrocities of Hiroshima and Nagasaki but still refers to the massacre of Chinese civilians in Nanjing as an "incident" (Strecher 1999, p. 295).

In this quote, Strecher points out the problem of selective memory and misinterpretation of the past as well as Murakami's attempt in his literary visions of historical events to deconstruct this deeply rooted narrative.

Before going into analysis of the war narratives of Murakami, I would like first to give a brief historical context for the events if not described directly but certainly referred to in the writer's books. The war-related narratives in Murakami's works evolve around the following points: Mukden (or Manchurian) Incident (1931), Nanking Massacre (1937) and Nomonhan Incident (1939). All three cast the Japanese military in a negative light, so it is no coincidence Murakami chooses exactly these events to base his critical narratives around. Furthermore, Murakami criticises not only the handling of the war strategy by the Japanese authorities but also the confusion of the post-war years induced by the officials of the state.

As I mentioned earlier, Murakami's political involvement and war critique starts with *A Wild Sheep Chase* (2002), where the title, as Sellers claims, reflects "the novel's theme: the futility of the individual struggle against faceless, nameless political entities" (Sellers 2017, p. 17). This struggle evokes Murakami's political metaphor of "the wall and the egg", which is easy to trace in the novel since the image of "the wall" (the System) is embodied in the mysterious and frightening figure of The Boss, whom Matthew Strecher calls "a manifestation of the postmodern State: hidden, elusive, and unaccountable" (Strecher 1998, p. 358). However, the focus of my attention here is on the history of Junitaki, which shows wartime Japan in its violent absurdity. One of the characters of this narrative is described as follows:

> [He] was particularly upset by these developments. He could not understand why such things as taxes and military service were at all necessary.
> "It seems to me things were better off like they used to be", he said (Murakami 2002, p. 241).

The history of the town Junitaki fits in the main historical discourse and, as Sellers explains, matches "the historically accurate actions of the Japanese government", which "used and misused" the ordinary citizens of the town (Sellers 2017, p. 19). Here it is possible to notice the first signs of the split in representing Japan – Japan the Military State, absurd and violent, indifferent to the needs of the citizens, and Japan of the ordinary people, the citizens who do not understand the actions of the authorities. This double-layered image of Japan as a wartime nation will reappear again in the further works of Murakami.

Murakami's next novel, which deals with the complicated issues of the Japanese past and war memory as part of the contemporary image of Japan and its identity, is *The Wind-Up Bird Chronicle* (2010), but since it has extensive and multi-layered war-related stories and has more significance for my research in its intertextual links to and direct influences on Mitchell's *Number9Dream* (2001), I would like to analyse it after giving a brief account of the representations of war-related violence in *Kafka on the Shore* (2006).

In his 2002 novel *Kafka on the Shore*, Murakami continues to create a narrative which presents a political critique of the wartime authorities. At the beginning of the novel, the author offers a description of the (fictional) event called "The Rice Bowl Hill Incident", which occurred on November 7th, 1944. The choice of the timeframe is not accidental. The country was in a critical state, on the verge of defeat, and the general mood permeates the schoolteacher's recollection of the events offered in the form of interviews documented by the American authorities and as personal letters to a psychiatrist. As mentioned earlier, Murakami implies that personal accounts of the events are much more reliable despite the possible subjectivity because 1) the military excluded some of the testimonies regarding the event; and 2) Okamichi, the schoolteacher herself, omitted a few personal details in her interview, which she confesses about in the letters to the doctor. The general description of the time is framed as follows: "The war wasn't going well, with the military retreating on the southern front, suicide attacks one after the other, air raids on cities getting worse all the time" (Murakami 2006b, p. 31). The critique of the military is represented in a tricky way since Murakami dismisses the whole notion of the military in general, claiming through his character that there is little difference between Japanese and American military authorities: "The military's always the same, whether Japanese or American" (Murakami 2006b, p. 97). Another military critique is voiced by the doctor:

> Frankly, I didn't like to work under military directions. In most cases their goals were strictly utilitarian... only arriving at conclusions that accorded with their preconceptions... But it was wartime and we couldn't very well say no. We had to keep quiet and do exactly as we were told. – Dr. Tsukayama (Murakami 2006b, p. 62).

In the doctor's words, the split between "them" and "us" as wartime Japanese is again noticeable. The lines suggest that "we" were forced by "them" and the responsibility lies fully with "them", while both "us" and "them" are clearly equal parts of the contemporary image of wartime Japan, and this split in representation is what makes the analysis all the harder.

"The Rice Bowl Hill Incident" describes the schoolteacher taking her elementary students to the forest on a quest for mushrooms (another feature of the wartime image – food was to be found in nature, and hunting for food was rendered more important than studies). The mushroom hunters notice the strange light in the skies but do not pay much attention to it – after all, combat aircraft bombing the cities were not an uncommon view. Due to the physiological issues, she has to face suddenly in the forest, Okamochi (the teacher) ends up beating one of her students, who drops unconscious as a result, and all his classmates follow his sad example.

This incident may be interpreted as a figurative representation of the relationship between Japan and its citizens: "In the end, the violence that Okamochi inflicts on Nakata metonymizes the violence inflicted by Japan on their civilians during World War II" (Sellers 2017, p. 40). Japan here is compared to a grown-up, who is supposed to take care of the children (citizens of Japan) in her charge, which she fails to do and gets violent towards them instead. The conclusion that follows is rather unsettling – the ordinary people of wartime Japan are portrayed (not only in *Kafka on the Shore*) as innocent victims who suffered themselves from the military regime. This fact complicates the understanding of the wartime image of Japan in Murakami's works. As James Orr, in his monography, *The Victim As Hero: Ideologies of Peace and National Identity in Postwar Japan* (2001), points out,

> Progressive texts, despite their insistence on recording Japan's past aggressions and rejecting war, encountered a problem in their construction of the Japanese people as an ethnic nation alienated from as well as victimized by the state: how was the people's struggle against their state to be transformed into the people's sovereignty within it? (Orr 2001, p. 104)

Orr formulates an important question which is particularly relevant to the research of the image of Japan since he implies the existence of "two Japans": Japan the state and Japan the people, which distorts the image. Murakami certainly goes as far as depicting Japan's wartime aggression and violence, but at the same time, it separates the people of Japan from it. This feature of Murakami's representation of wartime Japan manifests itself in his other works as well, among which *The Wind-Up Bird Chronicle* is one of the most significant.

One of the numerous research projects written on Murakami and his monumental work, *The Wind-Up Bird Chronicle* (2010), is called "a Chaucerian novel of interlocking narrators and narratives, each of which unsettles fixed ideas of Japanese history and identity" (Ellis et al. 2005, p. 550). While in its main plot, the novel follows Toru Okada on his quest to find his missing wife, through various parallel narratives, it can be read as a "complex treatment of Japan's violent military history of the last century" (Sellers 2017, p. 21). The events described in the novel concern Japan's actions in Manchuria, Nanking and Nomonhan.

Just as in his other novels described in this subchapter, here Murakami follows the mentioned events not from the position of official history and ideology but from the standpoint of personal memories, creating a "small narrative", which he contrasts to the "grand narratives" in terms of Lyotard (1984). In this regard, Rubin notes that "[r]ather than writing about historical facts… Murakami examines the Pacific War as a psychological phenomenon shared by generations of Japanese too young… to have experienced it first-hand" (Rubin 2002, p. 218). Thus, *The Wind-Up Bird Chronicle* becomes a work of interpretation of wartime events.

There are a lot of parallel narratives and "interlocking narrators" (Ellis et al. 2005, p. 550), but I am going to examine only those that have the most direct connection to war-related events, although, arguably, all of the narratives to some degree have a link or two to Japanese war past. In the centre of my attention, therefore, are the tales of Lieutenant Mamiya about his experiences on the continent, narrated both orally and in letters to Toru; Nutmeg's narrative about her father ("the veterinarian") and his involvement in "the two clumsy massacres" in Manchukuo; and Mr Honda's story about the Nomonhan Incident.

The start of Lieutenant Mamiya's story can be dated as 1937, when he was brought to Manchuria as part of the army. On a special mission, he goes to Mongolia, where the enemy catches him. He escapes death by choosing to go willingly into the dried well in the desert. After a while, he is saved by Lieutenant Honda. After that, his life is not the same. He tries to die during the war years while he is in the army and later in the Siberian camps, but somehow, he always survives, unlike all of his family.

Lieutenant Mamiya's narrative represents the hardships, losses and traumas which many Japanese had to face during the war years. In this tale, implicit is the criticism of the Japanese state, which led the nation into such conditions. Military action is also heavily criticised in the novel, deemed meaningless and absurd. One of the characters, a soldier who took part in the wartime events on the continent, confesses: "We did some terrible things in Nanking. My own unit did. We threw dozens of people into a well and dropped hand grenades in after them. Some of the things we did I couldn't bring myself to talk about" (Murakami 2010c, p. 143). The absurdity of the war is underlined in his comment: "This one war that doesn't have any Righteous Cause. It's just two sides killing each other. ... I can't believe that killing these people is going to do Japan one bit of good" (Murakami 2010c, p. 143). Another portion of the war critique comes out of Mamiya, who is confused and bewildered with the necessity to fight in Manchuria, which is not even his homeland:

> Why did we have to risk our lives to fight for this barren piece of earth devoid of military or industrial value, this vast land where nothing lived but wisps of grass and biting insects. To protect my homeland, I too would fight and die. But it made no sense to me at all to sacrifice my one and only life for the sake of this desolate patch of soil (Murakami 2010c, p. 146).

Mamiya's argument implies some patriotic meanings, but it is also clear that he does not consider Manchuria a good enough reason to fight and die for.

As Sellers points out, "Murakami's treatment of the Japanese military and its exploits on the continent concentrates on the blatant disregard for individual life and its value" (Sellers 2017, p. 26). To underline even further the absurdity of the war, Murakami describes the secret mission Mamiya is sent on. He witnesses the torture and death of his companions, and in the end, the mission fails all the same. Thus, according to Murakami's design, all the terrors of the war are meaningless in the end, and all the deaths are in vain.

Another component of the image of wartime Japan is "pseudo-bushido" ethics which is also used by Mitchell in *Number9Dream*. In Honda's narrative, Murakami describes the military practices of forced suicides: "Some officers had, on their own initiative, ordered their troops to retreat to avoid annihilation; their superiors forced them to commit suicide" (Murakami 2010c, p. 53). Murakami's position towards the military becomes clear through the abovementioned lines.

The story of The Two Clumsy Massacres, told by Nutmeg, is about Nutmeg's father, who is also called "veterinarian" in the text and who also took part in military actions on the continent. The first massacre is about the killing of the animals while leaving the town under the pretext that in such a way, they spare the animals their significant suffering. The second massacre follows the first one: the Japanese soldiers kill eight Chinese men. Both cases present acts of absurd violence, a fact that does not escape the commanding officer, who, nonetheless, follows the orders to the letter: "I think the order stinks. What the hell good is it going to do to kill these guys?... We've already killed a lot of Chinese, and adding a few bodies to the count isn't going to make any difference" (Murakami 2010c, p. 518). Especially ugly and violent in the description of this case is his order to break the skull of one of the Chinese with a baseball bat: "Orders are orders, I'm a soldier, and I have to follow orders" (Murakami 2010c, p. 518). Interestingly enough, this motif will repeat itself in the last novel of Murakami (for the present day), *Killing Commendatore* (2018[8]), where one of the characters is "forced to behead a Chinese prisoner" (Murakami 2018, p. 395), which causes his subsequent suicide.

The story of the two massacres becomes a sort of metaphor for representing Japanese violence on the continent during the war. In comparison, this can in no way be compared to Nanking Massacre; however, it frames Murakami's position toward killings in general. For him, it does not matter how many defenceless people (or even animals, for that matter) were wrongfully killed in order to call it a massacre. The author develops this theme in *Killing Commendatore* (2018) as well, addressing Nanking Massacre and stating through his character the following:

> Historians disagree on exactly how many died, but no one can deny that a massive number of noncombatants were sucked into the conflict and

---

[8] The given date is of the English edition, not the original novel in Japanese, published in 2017.

lost their lives. Some say 400,000, others 100,000. But what difference is there really between 400,000 lives and 100,000? (Murakami 2018, p. 396)

The humanitarian position of the writer is undeniable, thus, since he even counts killing eight people and eight animals as a massacre and a case of absurd violence.

All those war narratives in *The Wind-Up Bird Chronicle* may at first seem to have nothing to do with the central line of narration – Toru Okada. While listening to all the stories conveyed to him by various characters, he comes to understand how everything is connected though he is not sure what it all has to do with him:

All of these events were linked as in a circle, at the center of which stood prewar Manchuria, continental East Asia, and the short war of 1939 in Nomonhan. But why Kumiko and I should have been drawn into this historical chain of cause and effect I could not comprehend. All of these events had occurred long before Kumiko and I were born (Murakami 2010c, p. 498).

However, for a careful reader, it is possible to presume that Toru's own story, enriched by all the parallel narratives, "symbolizes the endeavor to understand oneself as a Japanese grounded historically in the hidden past" (Lo 2004, p. 270). It is also clear that, through Toru, Murakami demonstrates his own position on war, responsibility and identity. When asked in one of the interviews about the reasons for modern Japanese take responsibility for the actions and crimes committed by the previous generations, Murakami unambiguously replies:

Because we're Japanese. When I read about the atrocities in China in some books, I can't believe it. It's so stupid and absurd and meaningless. That was the generation of my father and grandfather. I want to know what drove them to do those kinds of things, to kill or maim thousands and thousands of people. I want to understand, but I don't (Murakami 2010c, p. 20).

Ultimately, both for Toru and Murakami himself (as for many Japanese), the sense of identity and self-image seems impossible without fully understanding their own past.

In her in-depth analysis of *The Wind-Up Bird Chronicle*, Sellers sums up the main direction and purpose of the depictions of the wartime violence in the novel:

Murakami uses *The Wind-Up Bird Chronicle* to undermine and criticize the widely accepted narratives about Japan's involvement on the continent.

His depictions of violence, buoyed by constant interjections about warfare's futility, emphasize the sense that contemporary Japan has forgotten the horrors of its past (Sellers 2017, p. 34).

In such a way, through the act of remembrance, the contemporary image of Japan – the image of Japan that reconstructs and revaluates its past – is created in *The Wind-Up Bird Chronicle*. The topic proves to be important to the author since he returns to it in his following novels, especially in *Killing Kommendatore*, which sort of "recycles" in many ways the main themes and motifs of *The Wind-Up Bird Chronicle*.

Killing Commendatore (2018) certainly seeks to recreate fictionalised historical narratives already employed by Murakami in his earlier novels. The novel parallels the events in Europe during World War II (mainly the annexation of Austria and the Kristallnacht massacre) and the Nanking Massacre in China. Like Murakami's other big works, the novel combines multiple narratives, which can roughly be divided into two timeframes: present and wartime. The present-time narrative revolves around a portrait painter who, during the novel, remains unnamed. His wife leaves him, and he deals with personal issues, first setting out on a long road trip and then finding a home at his friend's house in the mountains. The house belongs to the friend's father, who is a famous artist who led a life of a recluse and now suffers from dementia in a nursery home. The wartime narrative tells the story of this artist, named Tomohiko Amada, whose student years are spent in Austria during the German annexation of World War II while his younger brother Tsuguhiko takes part in the Nanking Massacre at the same time and kills himself soon after he returns home. For the purposes of this research, I will focus on the war-related narrative.

If the present-time narrative is told from the first perspective – Murakami returns to the techniques he used so often in his first novels – the wartime narrative featuring Tomohiko and Tsuguhiko is gathered by the protagonist from the following sources: through articles in the art books he gets in the local library; through the conversation-interviews with his friend Masahiko, Tomohiko Amada's son; through the reports he gets from Menshiki, protagonist's neighbour, a man of significant means, who conducts his own private investigation; and, finally, through Commendatore – an apparition who takes on a form of a white-bearded man from Amada's secret painting, whom only the protagonist can see and communicate with and who claims to be an idea or a metaphor. The protagonist becomes truly obsessed with the life story of Tomohiko Amada. The story gets retold many times by different narrators, and sometimes the crucial details differ from one account of an event to another. It seems Murakami implies that the ultimate truth the protagonist receives from Commendatore, the least reliable narrator in a normal sense, but probably because of that, the most reliable in the transcendent sense. The wartime narrative reaches the protagonist as a family myth, a collection of rumours gathered by the private investigator, a metaphor rather than a certainty, presenting in itself the same type of personal history with the unreliable narrator as opposed to the official histories which Murakami uses in his other novels.

Although there are two parallel war-related narratives in this novel – Tomohiko Amada in Austria and his involvement in the anti-Nazi resistance movement and Tsugihiko Amada's military experience in China – I am going to concentrate only on the story about Tsugihiko as part of my research of the image of Japan and representations of war violence. Tsugihiko's story is as follows: being the youngest son of an influential family, he studies music in a conservatory when he is drafted and sent to China, where he takes part in Nanking Massacre. At some point, he receives an order to decapitate a Chinese man with a sword, which he obeys. On his returning to Japan, instead of going back to the conservatory, he cuts his wrists and leaves a suicide note explaining everything he did in China. Through this narrative, Murakami explores the blind force of the military machine, its violence and its effect on the lives of ordinary Japanese again.

Critique of the System ("The Wall", in Murakami's words) is against the state and military authorities. When Masahiko describes how his uncle Tsugihiko was drafted due to a bureaucratic mistake despite being a student, he says: "But the army was grabbing any likely men they could find and dragging them in to be killed" (Murakami 2018, p. 393). The system here is presented as a powerful blind force, which, similar to a natural disaster, crushes individual will and fate. It is explained in the episode describing the order to kill a man with a sword: "It was unthinkable to refuse an order" (Murakami 2018, p. 399). Everyone was part of the system, which went back to the Emperor. In some sense, Murakami implies that the Emperor was The System: "An order from an officer in Japan's Imperial Army was an order from the Emperor himself" (Murakami 2018, p. 399). The criticism of the military and System also appears in the words of Masahiko, who reflects on what he would do if ordered to kill someone in the conditions of military actions violently:

> I might not be strong enough to stand up and say no if I were thrown into a system as violent as the military, even if I knew the order was horribly wrong or inhuman (Murakami 2018, p. 400).

The protagonist thinks to himself about the same matter and secretly doubts whether he could act in any different way in similar circumstances: "Would I be any different if I were in his uncle's shoes?" (Murakami 2018, p. 400). However, following such orders has its own horrible psychological consequences, as

Murakami shows in the example of Tsugihiko: "Uncle Tsuguhiko couldn't refuse his superior's order. ... He lacked the guts to do that. Yet later he was able to sharpen a razor and use it to kill himself" (Murakami 2018, p. 400). However, his suicide is interpreted in terms of protest against the system and not a weakness: "In that sense, I don't think he was weak at all. Only by taking his own life was my uncle able to recover his humanity" (Murakami 2018, p. 400). Tsugihiko prefers death to live in a state which allows such atrocities.

From the performed analysis, it is possible to conclude that Murakami remains faithful to himself when it comes to depicting wartime Japan. There are always overt and implicit critiques of the state machine, military, and The System represented through the personal stories of the ordinary Japanese whose lives are violently disrupted. The author creates "two Japans" – militaristic and suppressive authority, the State of Japan, and the suppressed victims, the people of Japan who follow the orders because "it was wartime and we couldn't very well say no" (Murakami 2006b, p. 62). Here there is a strong opposition between "them", the authorities, and "us", the people of Japan, the victims. The problem of this binary opposition remains unresolved even in Murakami's last novel. This split in the image of Japan with its ongoing dichotomy is particularly striking if compared to the modern image of the country that Murakami creates in his *Undergrounds*. By contrast, when analysing the religious violence, Murakami, as I demonstrated in the previous parts of this research, as a writer (and unlike his characters) seems to fully accept the "dark side" of Japan, admitting that the terrorists with their narratives and delusions are part of "us", "the Japanese".

3.7 Aesthetisation and Deconstruction of the Samurai Ethics in *Number9Dream*

If, by contrast, the theme of domestic violence in contemporary Japan as a component of its image has not become widespread in the works of Mitchell, the images of "traditional samurai ethics" / "pseudo-bushido" find their way into Mitchell's prose. Just as Murakami explores the images of historical violence, particularly in wartime Japan, Mitchell addresses the topic as well, though he does it in his own fashion. Mitchell's novels reveal the images of Japan that Murakami intentionally avoids – the images that adhere to the Western perspective, the images of "Western modernized Japan", "Japan without Fuji, cherry blossom or samurai". Unlike Murakami, Mitchell's visions of Japanese violence are occasionally associated with the ethics and aesthetics of samurai, which is most clearly manifested in the novel *Number9Dream*.

Among the stereotypical images of Japanese uniqueness (mono-ethnicity, ethnocentrism, collectivism, industriousness, hierarchy, specificity of the Japanese language picture of the world, aesthetic worldview, etc.), the most common are feminine cliché of geisha and cherry blossoms and masculine representations associated with the samurai spirit. The biased attitude of the West towards Japan, to a certain degree, has always been due to these images. In this regard, the researchers point out an interesting tendency: when the relations of the West with Japan are peaceful, the country of the rising sun in the media and literature is associated with female images, and during political or economic tension (as in the war years or the unexpected Westward economic upsurge in Japan) with military-related stereotypes. The Bushido Code of the Samurai becomes, in the present cultural context, a reference point for the changes taking place in society. In the cultural consciousness of the West, this code of honour is increasingly associated not with romantic ideas of a noble warrior, which is largely due to the romantic anachronism of the novels of the Japanese writer Mishima Yukio [9] but with inhumane cruelty. This stereotype became especially popular in the twentieth century after numerous wars in its first half, in which Japan actively participated, as well as the surprisingly fast economic growth of the country in the second half of the century. The latter caused some concerns in the West and made it possible for Western governments to look at the "yellow peril" from a different perspective, specifically economic when office workers started to be accepted as "samurais in costumes". Mitchell, as a Western author, cannot avoid such a stereotype as "samurai". However, he deconstructs the image of "samurai-like" Japan, highlighting new aspects of its "brutal" traits in the eyes of the West. The British writer illustrates several versions of the "samurai spirit" in the novel *Number9Dream*: one is related to the war images and another to the criminal (specifically, yakuza).

The "War" version is given in the chapter of *Number9Dream* titled "Kaiten". Eiji reads a diary written by his grandfather's older brother Subaru Tsukiyama, who participated in the Underwater Attack program called "Kaiten" during World War II. "Kaiten" is one of the programs in which submarine pilots were ordered to blast hostile ships at the cost of their own lives. According to Subaru Tsukiyama, the meaning of life is to defend the Motherland. He does not doubt the correctness of his choice. However, Eiji attempts to find out whether the victim of Subaru was in vain. From the diaries of Subaru, it is clear that he is aware of the false politics of his country, propaganda, and the inevitable defeat in the war, although official news suppressed the truth, "turning the very word into a taboo" (Mitchell 2001, p. 299). Here there is a critique of the state machine; however, Mitchell's characters, unlike Murakami's, do not place the

---

[9] The most striking examples are the well-known nationalist novel *Patriotism* (1966) as well as well-known tetralogy *The Sea of Fertility* (1968-1970), permeated with the nostalgic motives of the samurai past, beauty and death.

blame on the system, opposing "them" to "us" (I study this aspect of Murakami's works in the previous subchapter), fully accepting their responsibility. Subaru decides to go to the very end: "I believe the Kaiten Project is the reason I was born" (Mitchell 2001, p. 307), which may sound naïve but not victimised. A more critical version of the choice to go to the very end, to become a pilot-kamikaze, is announced by Subaru's arms mate Kusakabe, the one who reads the banned Shakespeare's books and admires the ponds in a Zen manner with Subaru, and does not exclude the possibility that in his previous life, he was a Buddhist wanderer monk (I analyse this character in the first chapter of this research). Kusakabe openly refuses to see the Americans as short-sighted and silly cowards, as offered by the official media sources of Japan, and later on, he boldly declares to Lieutenant Abe, who patriotically believes in the Righteous Cause of the war: "We have lost this war by swallowing our own propaganda" (Mitchell 2001, p. 305). The Lieutenant asks him why he chose to be part of the Kaiten project and to give up his life if he does not believe in victory and thinks that this war is all in vain and there is nothing more to defend. And the answer Kusakabe gives to the Lieutenant is what may be perceived as the echo of true samurai dignity: "The meaning of my sacrifice is to help Tokyo negotiate a less humiliating surrender" (Mitchell 2001, p. 305). Without believing in the false ideals of the System, Kusakabe believes himself to be part of Japan and is ready to do whatever is needed to protect it. The dichotomy between The State and the people so clearly manifested in Murakami's works is absent in Mitchell's.

In the representations of samurai culture in the novel, there is also Mitchell's bitter irony, which hints at the futility of the motto "for the sake of a new Japan", hiding behind the loss of samurai ideals in the new world in general. The final departure from the samurai values as it is depicted in the novel is a symbolic act committed by Eiji's father, who sells the sword, which has been in the family for generations. Eiji founds out about the sale from his paternal grandfather Takara Tsukiyama, Subaru Tsukiyama's younger brother (the very same Subaru who died during the war in the torpedo boat "Kaiten"). In Subaru's diary, given to Eiji by Takara Tsukiyama, Eiji, among other things, finds a touching passage addressed to Takara: "Live my life for me, Takara, and I will die your death for you" (Mitchell 2001, p. 312). The sword has been a family relic for five centuries, and thus Eiji's father (a person of dubious moral grounds) breaks away from the samurai past of his family and his country, bringing forth by this action the contemporary discourse on the relative role of belonging to a certain family or nation.

It is noteworthy that in Mitchell's *Number9Dream*, the carriers of samurai honour in modern Japan are the powerful criminal groups of the Yakuza, which incorporate cruelty and violence as the basis of their cultural codes. Yakuza is presented through Eiji's personal encounters with them when he looks for his father (protagonist's adventures with the leader of the Yakuza, who introduces the boy to a night-time Tokyo), as well as letters from Kozue Yamaya, who tells about the murder of his son and his own enslavement by Yakuza. Thus, it becomes possible to assume that if Eiji's fantasy and imagination are a tribute to the techno-Orientalist image of Japan, the events of his "real life" depict the reverse side of modern society, which includes criminal violence.

The image of Mitchell's representation of violence at first glance may seem like an indulgence in Western tastes for mass literature, the very same mass literature which is accustomed to seeing samurai's cruelty as one of the crucial components of the image of Japan. Nevertheless, the phenomena of the Yakuza in Mitchell's novel are shown as heirs of the samurai spirit in contemporary Japanese society. They complain that Japan allows itself to be so dependent on other countries and ignores its own traditional culture, lost its self-esteem, and only the yakuza now values and understands what really is Japanese. Eiji, begging the leader of the yakuza Morino to reveal to him the information about his father, asks how much he has to pay for it. Morino answers: "Why is it now money, money, money with kids nowadays? Little wonder Japan is becoming this moral and spiritual graveyard" (Mitchell 2001, p. 182).

Mitchell contrasts the image of Japan as a "spiritual graveyard" with the image embodied in the figure of yakuza leader Morino, who responds to Eiji's question by telling him that Eiji should pay with loyalty and respect, not money. Loyalty is considered one of the main principles of samurai culture. In this, we can trace a rather polemical representation of the yakuza as the bearers of the traditional values of the samurai culture, such as loyalty, self-sacrifice and generosity – the values that become small in a criminal world. The subtle irony of the traditional Japanese values lost in the modern world is shown in this correlation between the values of the bushido and the criminal world, as well as in the contrasting depiction of the understanding of these values by Tsukiyama Subaru, Kusakabe and yakuza. It is necessary to point out that Mitchell's critique is not directed at a stereotype related to the history of the spiritual culture of the military state but rather towards the modern ideological and cynical valorisation of the Bushido code in contemporary yakuza gangs. The killings and atrocities they commit through money and the division of spheres of influence, how they betray each other, reveal their inability to be the bearers of the mentioned values, the true representatives of the Japanese people. In modern Japan, most likely, the stereotype of the samurai spirit is a clear anachronism, and the emblematic examples – such as yakuza and pilot-kamikaze – are the basis for deconstructing stereotypes about the greatness of this spirit.

3.8 Conclusion

It can be summarized that David Mitchell and Murakami Haruki, in their respective novels, create the image of Japan, which includes the notion of a brutal nation which manifests its cruelty on various levels: religious, socio-political, criminal, and domestic/individual. Violence as a component of the image of Japan is divergent: it is aimed at ordinary Japanese (in a religious impulse to "purify and improve" the nation and the world or in a militaristic attempt to bring on the greatness of the nation by forcing millions of Japanese to die), certain criminal groups (murder for debts, division of spheres of the influence of Yakuza and enslavement of ordinary Japanese), and domestic violence. The most significant point of coincidence in the representation of the image of "violent Japan" was revealed during the analysis of the artistic understanding of the religious terror of "Aum Shinrikyo". The two authors create an almost identical ambivalent image of the terrorist act in Japan. However, a number of discrepancies in the representation of violence have also been analysed. David Mitchell, unlike Murakami Haruki, uses traditional exoticism but only to challenge stereotypical ideas about Japan. Mitchell points out the relevance of the representation of not only the exotic component of the image but also the acutely modern problems for the whole world. In their works, both writers ironically form a stereotypical image of Japan as a high-tech and, at times, brutal nation, which at some point reflects the present state of the world in general. As in the well-known classical examples of philosophical dystopia by William Golding, George Orwell, Kobo Abe, Komatsu Sakyo, and Shimada Masahiko, the locality (like England and Japan) loses its specificity, transforming itself into an image of the world in which humanity crisis propagates violence and cruelty, evolving into terror.

Conclusion

A contextual, typological and comparative approach to the study of the problem of the representation of Japan in contemporary culture and literature revealed a paradigm in the image of this country's national modes of representation in Murakami's and Mitchell's works. Comparative research has expanded the problematic range of studying the image of Japan, which from the mysterious and magical world created in the Western literature of the early twentieth century, transformed into a techno-orientalist nightmare (or "moral and spiritual graveyard", as Mitchell calls it).

It became clear that the works of Japanese writer Murakami Haruki are intertextually present in David Mitchell's "Japanese" novels, marking the key points of representation of the image of Japan and Japaneseness. The interaction of the semantic and poetic levels of the Japanese and English texts enables Mitchell to create an image of Japan from different national, cultural and artistic perspectives, as well as to broaden the horizon of representation of the foreign culture, exposing the revision of the various stereotypes about Japan and the Japanese national character. Mitchell, much similar to Murakami, does not exoticise Japan but shows "Japan as it is", creating a type of novel that he (Mitchell) calls the "bicultural novel", emphasising the balance of approaches – Japanese and non-Japanese.

In Mitchell's novels, Japanese themes are expressed in direct references to Murakami's works, which manifest themselves differently in the text. First of all, it is an open dialogue with Murakami, that is, a direct intersubjective interaction, seen not only in the conscious borrowing (often polemical) of semantics and elements of poetics but also in-text inclusion of the images that Murakami uses in his books. This sophisticated creative dialogue-polemic is built on the postmodern technique of confrontaitment (confrontation + entertainment), which is used in contemporary political discussions and reveals the peculiarities of the representation of Japan's image. In addition to this direct intersubjective interaction, Mitchell's works implement an intertextual space without explicit postmodern collage-like references to Japanese images of Murakami's novels. Both Mitchell and Murakami develop new approaches to representing Japan. Unlike traditional exotic descriptiveness, the authors have created new strategies for representing Japan not just as a country foreign to the West but "just like us".

The Japanese world of Murakami is manifested on various levels of Mitchell's novels: in the word and genre games, the play in the development of such "Murakami" and general features of postmodern literature as lightness, "superficiality" with the simultaneous disclosure of eternal themes, the search for love in the maze of one's self, dream-life, reality-illusion). For Mitchell, who knows and admires Japan, Murakami's work becomes an important intertextual resource and an incentive to redefine the image of contemporary Japan and Japanese nationality formed in the literary tradition.

Mitchell's work may be thought unoriginal because of the imitation of Murakami or portrayal of Japan in the techno-orientalist style of the cyberpunk genre. However, as Nihei (2009) rightly points out, Mitchell's use of multiple subjectivities, including the Japanese perspective (Japanese protagonist's worldview), as well as his attempt to dramatically change the traditional Western image of Japan, is quite unique in contemporary world literature.

Mitchell, having created a remedial transcultural image of Japan, achieved his goal of writing a transcultural novel and changing views on Orientalism. These clearly stated goals were the subordinate artistic development of the image of Japan in his novels. Structuring such an image of Japan and Japaneseness gives reason to see in Mitchell's works an outlet for knowledge of what contemporary Japan and Japanese are. Such a move beyond the ethnocentric, Orientalist understanding of the representation of the image of Japan and the Japanese hero allows one to see in Mitchell's novel a new modern image of Japan in the aspect of East-West dialogue.

In his novels, Mitchell applies a new narrative principle: the story in the English text about Japan is narrated from the standpoint of the cultural and ethnic Other (in regards to the cultural identity of the author of the text). The effect that Murakami achieves through the introduction of Western elements into the text and distancing himself from traditional Japanese symbols, Mitchell creates otherwise – through excessive immersion in Japanese socio-political and cultural realities and excessive hyperbolisation, bringing the stereotype to the level of parody. For instance, if the image of *sakura* ironically indicates a biased vision of Japan by Europeans, then the image of yakuza emerges as a downside of Japanese society. Murakami also writes about this, referring to the images of World War II and the aggressive policies of Japan, as well as thematising the events of the Sarin attack in his works. Such political urgency contributes to the deconstruction of the stereotypes of Japan's exoticism. In contrast to stereotypical, one-line, plane images, Murakami, in a rather postmodern way, represents the image of Japan in its historical dynamics and through universal humanistic values. The human existence presented in Mitchell's *Number9Dream* also destroys the negative ethnic stereotypes.

Stereotypes are known to dictate a static, holistic, unified and linear vision of reality, while postmodern discourse renounces the uniqueness of sustainable national-cultural ideas. In addition, cultural stereotypes create a convenient picture of the world where the "I" can freely perceive and speak of the Other in the so-called objective line, as evidenced by old Orientalist traditions which find its expression in Puccini's *Madam Butterfly*, as well as in the works of Lottie and Benedict). Contrarily, Mitchell chooses a Japanese point of view for his narrative to deconstruct stereotypical perceptions of Japan. In doing so, Mitchell goes beyond both classical orientalism and the new direction of techno-orientalism, parodying his own images, which, of course, also relate to the ironic-game technique of Murakami's novels.

Mitchell's creative reception of Murakami's works forms the basis for Japan's meta-image (self-referential image), including the fantasy level of representation as well. Mitchell's and Murakami's creativity testifies to the impossibility of relying on a "pure experience" called "Japan", which, if one continues the Roland Barthes metaphor of the "empire of signs" (Barthes 1983), is embedded in the multichannel transcultural discourse of the present.

The comparative analysis of English and Japanese works performed in this book reveals both deep analogies and differences in the representation of the image of Japan, actualizing the national specificity of the texts. The analysis allows for distinguishing the connecting sphere between Western and Eastern cultures in the parameters of "active dialogical understanding" as "inclusion in a dialogical context" (Bakhtin 1979, p. 381).

A comparative study of the works of Murakami and Mitchell undertaken in the three chapters of this research gives grounds for the following conclusions. The first chapter of this book shows that the extended and diverse imagological specification of the image of Japan (such as Fuji and cherry blossoms) defines the modern image of the country, opposing the stereotypical image of the distant exotic East. Therefore, a comparative analysis of the "Japanese" novels of Mitchell as well as the works of Murakami Haruki reveal a range of problems involving the dichotomy of East-West perceptions and show how the writers construct images of Japan from the viewpoint of both foreigners and Japanese, respectively. One of the characteristics of Murakami's fiction, apart from being "deadpan" and lacking emotion/sentimentalism, is, on a certain level, being "mimetic". Murakami describes bored people as representing modern Japan (also argued by Suzuki, 2004 and Suter, 2011) and simultaneously sharing the atmosphere with the reader. Murakami does not use stereotypical icons of Japaneseness. It can be debated that Murakami, through his careful references to popular culture and especially popular music, recreates in his writing the atmosphere of modern Japan and the modern world that is more resonant to the reader than a traditional culture would be. Mitchell, on the other hand, does not try to avoid stereotypes in his novels. Nevertheless, he uses them playfully, in a postmodern ironic and parodic fashion, deconstructing them by doing so. Both Mitchell and Murakami share the feature of the accentuation of cultural and historical changes regarding the views on Japan and Japaneseness refusing to follow cultural and ethnocentric concepts developed long ago. In the works of both of the authors, not only is revealed the question of what it means to be Japanese in a modern globalised society, but also what it means to be human.

As it was proven in the second chapter of this book, narrative techniques and the semantics of the images of Japan and Japaneseness created by Mitchell and Murakami demonstrate the obvious connection with the techno-orientalist model of the image of Japan. Techno-orientalism is known to be a combination of the images of high technology and anachronistic images of exotic Japan, and in the novels of Murakami and Mitchell, among other various representations of Japan, it is possible to find the techno-images, too. Information networks and spaces are combined with an exotic urban landscape, creating a somewhat cyberpunk representation of metropolitan Tokyo. Techno-orientalist poetics of Mitchell's novels are a kind of encyclopaedia on parody and pastiche about cyberpunk, continuous quotation of cross-referential and techno-orientalist images. This technique has much in common with the works of contemporary writers in the East and the West, such as *Neuromancer* by William Gibson, *The Dream Messenger* (*Yumezukai*) by Shimada Masahiko, *Paprika* by Tsutsui Yasutaka and so on. Both Mitchell and Murakami find a new way of representing futuristic Japan without making it too fantastic and "science fiction", showing it in more realistic ways. It still would be fair to say that Murakami is far less concerned about "high tech" than Mitchell and that Murakami's representation of "urban life" predates and does not heavily rely on "techno-orientalist" views of Japan.

The third chapter discloses the violent dimensions of the image of Japan in the works of Mitchell and Murakami. Violence in their works manifests itself on various levels: religious, historical, socio-political, criminal, and domestic/individual. The most significant point of coincidence in the representation of the image of "violent Japan" was revealed during the analysis of the artistic understanding of the religious terror of "Aum Shinrikyo". The two authors create an almost identical ambivalent image of the terrorist in Japan (The Tokyo Subway sarin attack, 1995), though using different narrative strategies. Murakami addresses the problem in his journalistic investigation and collection of non-fiction interviews with the victims and participants of the terror act. Mitchell, by contrast, creates a fictional character who faces the attack and takes part in it. A number of discrepancies in the representation of violence have also been analysed. Mitchell, unlike Murakami, uses traditional exoticisms but only to challenge stereotypical ideas about Japan. In their works, both writers ironically form a stereotypical image of Japan as a high-tech and, at times, brutal nation, which acquires the general meaning of the present state of the world as a whole. Thus, the locality of Japan loses its specificity,

Conclusion

transforming itself into an image of the world in which the humanity crisis propagates violence and cruelty, evolving into terror.

In the works of both authors, the intent to depict a new world of Japan stripped of traditional stereotypical traits becomes clear. Studying the representations of Japan and Japanese national character helps to understand the role of Murakami and Mitchell in the formation of a new image of Japan, the de-stereotyping of anachronistic ideas about Japanese national exclusivity, sacrificial patriotism, militaristic aggression etc., enriching by doing so the world literature with new visions of the country and its culture. This motive of deconstruction of the stereotypical national images is not unique to just Murakami's and Mitchell's works but rather common to the whole world of literature. Nationality is no longer the dominant principle of creating or reinventing the image of a certain country in a work of literature. Therefore, Japan in Murakami and Mitchell is a place where any person identified by a certain set of similar features lives. The new type of character navigates in this world with ease but continues to be lonely and constantly searches for his or her place and identity. What Washburn rightly says about Murakami's protagonist – "the detached, occasionally naïve, coolly sceptical young man" (Washburn 2007, p. 244) – we can equally apply to Mitchell's characters as well. The protagonists are disconnected from reality around them, thus creating their identity regardless of social roles, national features or historical heritage. In such a way, the new image of Japan emerges; paradoxical in its ambiguity, it is well in line with the worldwide general tendency to attempt to re-identify itself.

References

Bakhtin, M. (1979). K Metodologii Gumanitarnykh Nauk . In: *Estetika Slovesnogo Tvorchestva*. Moscow: Iskusstvo.

Banks, I. (2008). *Canal Dreams*. London: Hachette UK.

Barns, J. (2011). *Metroland*. New York: Knopf Doubleday Publishing Group.

Barthes, R. (1983). *The Empire of Signs*. Translated by J. Cape. New York: Hill and Wang.

Basho, M. (2003). Frog Haiku. In: *A Zen Wave: Bashô's Haiku and Zen*. [online] Berkeley, California: Shoemaker & Hoard, p.154. Available at: http://www.bopsecrets.org/gateway/passages/basho-frog.htm [Accessed 5 May 2020].

Baudrillard, J. (1988). *Selected Writings (of) Jean Baudrillard*. Translated by M. Poster. Stanford (Calif.) Stanford University Press.

Baudrillard, J. (1994a). *Simulacra and Simulation*. [online] *Google Books*. University of Michigan Press. Available at: https://books.google.co.jp/books/about/Simulacra_and_Simulation.html?id=yKNPnQAACAAJ&redir_esc=y [Accessed 12 May 2023].

Baudrillard, J. (1994b). *The Illusion of the End*. Translated by C. Turner. Cambridge: Polity Press.

Benedict, R. (1967). *The Chrysanthemum and the Sword*. Houghton Mifflin Harcourt.

Beppu, H. (1987). *Ideorogi Toshite No Nihonjin-ron*. Tokyo: Shis no kagaku-sha.

Bolter, J.D. and Grusin, R. (2003). *Remediation: Understanding New Media*. Cambridge, Mass.: Mit Press.

Bourdain, A. (2002). *Cooks Tour*. Bloomsbury Publishing Plc.

Buruma, I. (1996). Becoming Japanese. *The New Yorker*, 1 (December 23 & 30, 1996 Issue), p.60.

Childs, P. and Green, J. (2011). The Novels in Nine Parts. In: S. Dillon, ed., *David Mitchell: Critical Essays*. Gylphi Limited, pp.25–49.

Critchley, S. (2008). Violence, By Slavoj Zizek. A dream of divine violence. *The Independent*. [online] Available at: https://www.independent.co.uk/arts-entertainment/books/reviews/violence-by-slavoj-zizek-769535.html [Accessed 12 Dec. 2022].

Dale, P.N. (1986). *The Myth of Japanese Uniqueness Revisited*. Oxford: Nissan Institute Of Japanese Studies.

Davis, S.P. and Yosomono, E. (2012). *6 WTF Japanese Trends (You Can Blame on White Guys)*. [online] Cracked.com. Available at: https://www.cracked.com/article_19098_6-wtf-japanese-trends-you-can-blame-white-guys.html [Accessed 12 Dec. 2022].

DeLillo, D. (1989). *Americana*. Penguin Books.

Derrida, J. (1985). Letter to a Japanese Friend. In: W. David and B. Robert, eds., *Derrida and Differance*. Parousia Press.

Derrida, J. and Caputo, J.D. (1997). *Deconstruction in a nutshell: a conversation with Jacques Derrida*. New York: Fordham University Press.

Dyserinck, H. (2003). Imagology and the Problem of Ethnic Identity. *Scholarly Review of the International Association of Intercultural Studies*, 1(1 Spring), pp. 1–8.

Ellis, J., Hirabayashi, M. and Murakami, H. (2005). In Dreams Begins Responsibility: An Interview with Haruki Murakami. *The Georgia Review*, 59(3), pp. 548–567.

Erchak, G.M. (1992). *The Anthropology of Self and Behavior*. New Brunswick, N.J.: Rutgers University Press.

Fish, S. (2002). Can Postmodernism Condemn Terrorism? Don't Blame Relativism. *The Responsive Community*, 1(Summer), pp.27–31.

Geertz, C. (1988). *Works and Lives: the Anthropologist as Author*. Cambridge: Polity.

Gibson, W. (1984). *Neuromancer*. London: Harper/Voyager.

Goldsmith, O. (2018). *The Citizen of the World Or Letters from a Chinese Philosopher, Residing in London, to His Friend in the East*. Creative Media Partners, LLC.

Hassan, I. (1987). Toward a Concept of Postmodernism. In: *The Postmodern Turn: Essays in Postmodern Theory and Culture*. Columbus, Ohio: Ohio State University Press, pp.84–96.

Hassan, I. (1988). Quest for the Subject: The Self in Literature. *Contemporary Literature*, 29(3), pp.420–437. doi:https://doi.org/10.2307/1208455.

Hoffmann, G. (2005). *From Modernism to Postmodernism: Concepts and Strategies of Postmodern American Fiction*. Amsterdam: Rodopi, New York.

Huisman, M. (2011). *Orientalism and the Spectacle of the Other*. Master Thesis – Media, Culture & Society. Erasmus University Rotterdam [online] Available at: https://thesis.eur.nl/pub/10968/ [Accessed 25 May 2023].

Iwabuchi, K. (1994). Complicit Exoticism: Japan and Its Other. *Continuum*, 8(2), pp.49–82. doi:https://doi.org/10.1080/10304319409365669.

Iwabuchi, K. (2002). *Recentering Globalization: Popular Culture and Japanese Transnationalism*. Duke University Press.

Jameson, F. (1993). *Postmodernism, or, the Cultural Logic of Late Capitalism*. London: Verso.

Johnson, S.K. (2001). *The Japanese through American Eyes*. Stanford, Calif.: Stanford Univ. Press.

Karatani, K. (1989). One Spirit, Two Nineteenth Centuries. In: M. Miyoshi and H.D. Harootunian, eds., *Postmodernism and Japan*. Durham, pp.259–272.

Karatani, K. (1993). *Origins of Modern Japanese Literature*. Durham: Duke University Press.

Karatani, K. (1999a). Edo Exegesis and the Present. In: M. Marra, ed., *Modern Japanese Aesthetics: a Reader*. University of Hawaii Press, pp.263–299.

Karatani, K. (1999b). Murakami Haruki's Landscape. In: Y. Kuritsubo and T. Tsuge, eds., *Murakami Haruki Studies, 01*. Tokyo: Wakakusa Shobo, pp.296–306.

Karatani, K. (2011). *History and Repetition*. Columbia University Press.

Kipling, R. (2021). The Ballad of East and West. *The Kipling Society*. [online] Available at: https://www.kiplingsociety.co.uk/poem/poems_eastwest.htm [Accessed 12 Dec. 2022].

Lesser, J. (2014). *Get Yourself Connected: Time, Space, and Character Networks in David Mitchell's Fiction*. [Theses and Dissertations] Available at: https://

via.library.depaul.edu/cgi/viewcontent.cgi?article=1178&context=etd [Accessed 12 Dec. 2022].

Lewis, A. (2013). *The Essence of the Japanese Mind: Haruki Murakami and the Nobel Prize.* [online] lareviewofbooks.org. Available at: https://lareviewofbooks.org/article/the-essence-of-the-japanese-mind-on-haruki-murakami-and-the-nobel-prize/ [Accessed 12 Dec. 2019].

Lie, J. (2004). *Multiethnic Japan.* Cambridge, Mass.; London: Harvard University Press.

Littlewood, I. (2007). Japan. In: M. Beller and J. Leerssen, eds., *Imagology: the cultural construction and literary representation of national characters: a critical study.* Rodopi.

Lo, K.-C. (2004). Return to What One Imagines to Be There: Masculinity and Racial Otherness in Haruki Murakami's Writings about China. *Novel: A Forum on Fiction,* 37(3), pp.258–276. doi:https://doi.org/10.1215/ddnov.037030258.

Lotman, Y. (1998). Tekst v Tekste. In: *Ob iskusstve.* Saint Petersburg: Iskusstvo, pp.423–436.

Lozano-Mendez, A. (2010). Techno-orientalism in East-Asian Contexts: Reiteration, Diversification, Adaptation. In: M. Telmissany and T. Schwartz, eds., *Counterpoints: Edward Said's Legacy.* New York: Publisher, pp.183–206.

Lyotard, J.-F. (1984). *The Postmodern Condition a Report on Knowledge.* Manchester Univ. Press.

McInerney, J. (1992). Roll Over Basho: Who Japan Is Reading, and Why. *The New York Times.* [online] 27 Sep. Available at: https://www.nytimes.com/1992/09/27/books/roll-over-basho-who-japan-is-reading-and-why.html [Accessed 12 Dec. 2022].

McLeod, K. (2013). Afro-Samurai: Techno-Orientalism and Contemporary Hip Hop. *Popular Music,* 32(2), pp.259–275. doi:https://doi.org/10.1017/s0261143013000056.

McLuhan, M. (1962). *The Gutenberg Galaxy: the Making of Typographic Man.* London: Routledge And Kegan Paul.

McLuhan, M. (1973). *Understanding Media.* London: Sphere Books.

Mitchell, D. (2001). *Number9Dream.* London: Spectre.

Mitchell, D. (2003). *Japan and My Writing.* [online] randomhouse.com. Available at: http://www.randomhouse.com/boldtype/1100/mitchell/essay.html [Accessed 2 Aug. 2022].

Mitchell, D. (2007a). *Ghostwritten.* Knopf Doubleday Publishing Group.

Mitchell, D. (2007b). *Somewhere between History and the Imagination. British Novelist David Mitchell Talks about His New book, Japan and the Butterfly Effect of Fiction.* [online] *https://www.japantimes.co.jp/.* 24 Jun. Available at: https://www.japantimes.co.jp/culture/2007/06/24/books/book-reviews/somewhere-between-history-and-the-imagination/#.XfHjX-gzZRZ [Accessed 12 Dec. 2022].

Mitchell, D. (2010). *David Mitchell, The Art of Fiction No. 204.* [online] *The Paris Review. No 193.* Available at: https://www.theparisreview.org/interviews/6034/david-mitchell-the-art-of-fiction-no-204-david-mitchell [Accessed 12 Dec. 2022].

Mitchell, D. (2011). *An Interview with David Mitchell*. [online] *https://www.book browse.com/*. 28 Feb. Available at: https://www.bookbrowse.com/author_interviews/full/index.cfm/author_number/480/david-mitchell [Accessed 12 Dec. 2022].

Mitchell, D. (2014). *David Mitchell Interview*. [online] *Indiebound.org*. Available at: https://www.indiebound.org/author-interviews/mitchelldavid [Accessed 12 Dec. 2022].

Miyoshi, M. (1991). *Off Center: Power and Culture Relations between Japan and the United States*. Cambridge, Mass.: Harvard University Press.

Montesquieu , C. (2008). *Persian Letters*. OUP Oxford.

Morley, D. and Robins, K. (1995). Techno-Orientalism: Japan Panic. In *Spaces of Identity: Global Media, Electronic Landscapes and Cultural Boundaries*. London, New York: Routledge, pp.147–173.

Murakami, H. (1988). *Dansu dansu dansu*. Tokyo: K dansha.

Murakami, H. (1991). *Noruei no mori*. Tokyo: K dansha.

Murakami, H. (1993). A Slow Boat to China. Translated by A. Birnbaum. In: *The Elephant Vanishes*. New York: Vintage Books, pp.217–240.

Murakami, H. (1994a). *Neji maki dori kuronikuru*. Tokyo: Shinch sha.

Murakami, H. (1994b). The Conversation: Haruki Murakami. *Tokyo Journal*, August(1), p.20.

Murakami, H. (1997a). *Neji maki dori kuronikuru*. Tokyo: Shinch sha.

Murakami, H. (1997b). *Neji maki dori kuronikuru*. Tokyo: Shinch sha.

Murakami, H. (1999). Mejirushi no nai akumu. In: *And guraundo*. Tokyo: K dansha, pp.733–777.

Murakami, H. (2002). *A wild sheep chase*. 1st Vintage International ed. ed. Translated by A. Birnbaum. New York: Vintage Books.

Murakami, H. (2004). *Kaze-no uta wo kike*. Tokyo: K dansha.

Murakami, H. (2006a). *Afut d ku*. Tokyo: K dansha .

Murakami, H. (2006b). *Kafka on the shore*. 1st Vintage International ed. ed. Translated by P. Gabriel. New York: Vintage International.

Murakami, H. (2007). *After dark*. Translated by J. Rubin. Knopf Doubleday Publishing Group.

Murakami, H. (2009a). *And guraundo* . Tokyo: K dansha .

Murakami, H. (2009b). *Murakami Haruki-shi: '1Q84' wo kataru* . *Mainichishinbun 17 Sept*. 17 Sep.

Murakami, H. (2009c). *The Novelist in Wartime*. [online] Salon. Available at: https://www.salon.com/2009/02/20/haruki_murakami/ [Accessed 13 Dec. 2022].

Murakami, H. (2010a). *Dance Dance Dance*. Translated by A. Birnbaum. Knopf Doubleday Publishing Group.

Murakami, H. (2010b). *Norwegian Wood*. Translated by J. Rubin. Knopf Doubleday Publishing Group.

Murakami, H. (2010c). *The Wind-Up Bird Chronicle*. Translated by J. Rubin. Knopf Doubleday Publishing Group.

Murakami, H. (2010d). *Underground: The Tokyo Gas Attack and the Japanese Psyche*. Translated by A. Birnbaum. and Translated by P. Gabriel. Knopf Doubleday Publishing Group.

Murakami, H. (2013). *1Q84: novel*. Translated by J. Rubin. and Translated by P. Gabriel. New York, N.Y.: Vintage Books.

Murakami, H. (2016). *Hear the Wind Sing*. VINTAGE.

Murakami, H. (2017a). *Kishidanch goroshi*. Tokyo: Shinch sha.

Murakami, H. (2017b). *Kishidanch goroshi*. Tokyo: Shinch sha.

Murakami, H. (2018). *Killing Commendatore*. Translated by P. Gabriel. And Translated by T. Goosen. London: Harvill Secker.

Murakami, H. (2019a). *'Kaminokodomotachihaminaodoru' intaby `Murakami Haruki-san no sh setsu wa, hitotsuhitotsu no kotoba ni imi ga arukara / 'All God's Children Dance' Interview 'In Haruki Murakami's novels, each word has a meaning'*. [online] enterstage.jp. 14 May. Available at: https://enterstage.jp/interview/2019/05/011925.html [Accessed 10 May 2023].

Murakami, H. (2019b). *Questions for Murakami about Kafka on the Shore*. [online] http://www.harukimurakami.com/. Available at: http://www.harukimurakami.com/resource_category/q_and_a/questions-for-haruki-murakami-about-kafka-on-the-shore [Accessed 13 Dec. 2022].

Murakami, H. (2019c). *Sh setsuka 40-nen to 'Kishidanch goroshi': Murakami Haruki-san tokubetsu intaby*. Nagasaki shinbun (3 May). 3 May.

Murakami, H. and Kawai, H. (2016). *Haruki Murakami Goes to Meet Hayao Kawai*. [online] *Google Books*. Daimon Verlag. Available at: https://books.google.co.jp/books/about/Haruki_Murakami_Goes_to_Meet_Hayao_Kawai.html?id=lERjvgAACAAJ&redir_esc=y [Accessed 12 May 2023].

Nakamura, H. (2012). 'In Dreams Begins Responsibility': Murakami, Yeats and Counterpoint in Écriture. *The International Journal of the Humanities: Annual Review*, 9(5), pp.299–308. doi:https://doi.org/10.18848/1447-9508/cgp/v09i05/58240.

Nakamura, L. (2002). *Cybertypes: Race, Ethnicity, and Identity on the Internet*. New York: Routledge.

Napier, S.J. (1996). *The Fantastic in Modern Japanese Literature: the Subversion of Modernity*. London: Routledge.

Nihei, C. (2009). Thinking outside the Chinese Box: David Mitchell and Murakami Haruki's subversion of stereotypes about Japan. *New Voices*, 3, pp.86–103. doi:https://doi.org/10.21159/nv.03.05.

O'Donnell, P. (2015). *A Temporary Future: the Fiction of David Mitchell*. New York: Bloomsbury Academic.

Orr, J.J. (2001). *The Victim as Hero: Ideologies of Peace and National Identity in Postwar Japan*. Hawaii: University of Hawaii Press.

Pirandello, L. (2016). *Six Characters in Search of an Author*. Bloomsbury Publishing.

Posadas, B.T. (2011). Remediation of 'Japan' in Nuber9Dreams. In: S. Dillon, ed., *David Mitchell: Critical Essays*. Gylphi Limited, pp.77–104.

Rosen, S.L. (2000). Japan as Other: Orientalism and Cultural Conflict. *Intercultural Communication*, [online] November(4). Available at: https://www.immi.se/intercultural/nr4/rosen.htm [Accessed 12 Dec. 2022].

Rubin, J. (2002). *Haruki Murakami and the Music of Words*. London: Harvill Press.

Said, E. (1979). *Orientalism*. New York: Random House.

Said, E. (1993). *Culture and Imperialism*. New York: Alfred Knopf.

Sakai, N. (1989). Modernity and Its Critique: The Problem of Universalism and Particularism. In: M. Miyoshi and H. Harootunian, eds., *Postmodernism and Japan*. Durham: Duke University Press, pp.93-122.

Schoene, B. (2009). *The Cosmopolitan Novel*. Edinburgh: Edinburgh University Press.

Sellers, B. (2017). *Down the Well: Embedded Narratives and Japanese War Memory in Haruki Murakami*. [online] Available at: https://trace.tennessee.edu/utk_chanhonoproj/2103 [Accessed 12 Dec. 2022].

Shakespeare, W. (2000). *The Tragedy of Macbeth*. Cambridge University Press.

Simpson, K. (2011). Or Something Like That: Coming of Age in Number9Dream. In: S. Dillon, ed., *David Mitchell: critical essays*, pp. 49-76.

Strecher, M.C. (1998). Beyond 'Pure' Literature: Mimesis, Formula, and the Postmodern in the Fiction of Murakami Haruki. *The Journal of Asian Studies*, 57(2), pp. 354–378.

Strecher, M.C. (1999). Magical Realism and the Search for Identity in the Fiction of Murakami Haruki. *Journal of Japanese Studies*, 25(2), pp. 263–298.

Suter, R. (2011). *The Japanization of Modernity: Murakami Haruki between Japan and the United States*. Boston, Mass.; London: Harvard University Asia Center.

Suzuki, A. (2004). Boredom of Postmodern World: The Paradigm of the Present Day for Japanese and American Literature and Art (On Haruki Murakami and David Lynch). *The Katahira*, 39(Mar 2004), p.pp. 101-114.

Tatsumi, T. (2002). The Japanoid Manifesto: Toward a New Poetics of Invisible Culture. *Review of Contemporary Fiction*, New Japanese Fiction-Vol. 22(2), pp.2–18.

Tatsumi, T. (2006). *Full Metal apache: Transactions between Cyberpunk Japan and Avant-Pop America*. Durham: Duke University Press.

Thornber, K.L. (2009). *Empire of Texts in Motion: Chinese, Korean, and Taiwanese Transculturations of Japanese Literature*. Cambridge, Mass.: Harvard University Asia Center.

Thornton, N.W. (1961). *The Bridge of San Luis Rey*. Penguin Books.

Wagenaar, W. (2016). Wacky Japan: A New Face of Orientalism. *Asia in Focus: A Nordic journal on Asia by early career researchers*, 1(3), pp.46–54.

Washburn, D.C. (2007). *Translating Mount Fuji: Modern Japanese Fiction and the Ethics of Identity*. New York, N.Y.: Columbia University Press.

Winter, M. (1985). Don Quichote und Frankenstein. Utopie als Utopiekritik: Zur Geneze der negativen Utopie. *Utopieforshung*, 3(1), pp.86–112.

Yomoto, I. (2006). Murakami Haruki To Eiga. In: M. Shibata, M. Numano, Fujii S. and I. Yomota, eds., *Sekai Wa Murakami Haruki Wo Dō Yomu Ka*. Bungeishunjū, pp.137–52.

Index

A

a leader of the sect, 55
alienation, 13
Americanized Japan, 19
Aum Shinrikyo, 45, 53
authentic, 29

B

Barthes, Roland, xi
Benjamin, Walter, 43
biases, ix, xi, 23
Bildungsroman, 11, 16
Blain, Michael, 43

C

Chrysanthemum and the Sword, 25
civil unrest, 44
clash of cultures, 20
cleansing Japan, 52
confrontaitment, 77
controversial image, xiv
creative reception, 79
crime and terror, 44
crisis of humanity, 50
cross-cultural communication, 25
cross-cultural interaction, ix
cultural cross-representation, 4
cultural differences, 20
cultural discourse, xiv
cultural logic of violence, 43
cultural uniqueness, x
cyberpunk, x, 26
cyberspace, 38

D

data dance, 40
deconstruction, 28
deconstruction of the stereotypes, xiii
deployment of the family theme, 16
Derrida, Jacques, xi
distant exotic East, 7
domestic violence, 45, 61

E

East-West cultural dialogue, xii
exotic image, ix

F

fundamentalism and regionalism, 49
futuristic image of Japan, xiv
futuristic Japan, 42

G

gas attack, 51
Ghostwritten, 4, 5, 6, 8, 9, 10, 12, 14, 15, 17, 19, 20, 21, 30, 33, 41, 50, 51, 52, 53, 57, 58, 85
Gibson, William, x, 32, 35, 40, 42, 80
global village, 9
globalization, ix, 20, 51
great Japanese myth, 25

H

Haruki, Murakami, x
heteroimage, 6
Historical violence, 61
human existence, 4, 14, 16, 22, 78
humanitarian crisis, 57

I

identity, xii, 4, 10, 11, 12, 14, 16, 20, 24, 26, 40, 45, 50, 51, 55, 63, 64, 66, 69, 78, 81
ideological prejudices, xiv
imagological experiment, 13
individual memory, 49
individual responsibility, 46
inner terror, 45
intercultural communication, 19
intercultural dialogue, ix
international conflict, 44
Intertextual Component, xiii
intertextual doppelganger, xiii, 30
intertextual space, 13
intertextuality, xii, xiii, 6, 8, 33, 59
ironic representation, 19
ironic way of depicting Japan, xv
Iwabuchi, Koichi, xi

J

Japan the people, 66
Japan the state, 66
Japanese character, 6, 17, 20, 33, 56
Japanese culture, ix, x
Japanese national identity, xi
Japanese terror, 53
Japaneseness, ix, xi, xii, xiii, 1, 2, 7, 11, 12, 16, 18, 19, 22, 26, 27, 29, 36, 40, 49, 77, 78, 79, 80
japanoid, 32

K

Karatani, Kojin, xi, xii
Koichi, Iwabuchi, xiii

L

linear vision of reality, 78
literary allusions, 4
literary concepts, 5
literary realism, xv
literary reality, xv
Lyotard, François, 62

M

magical realism, xv
Masao Miyoshi, xi
Masao, Miyoshi, xiii
mass culture, 43
Media, 29
mimetic, xv
minus-technique, 18
misconceptions, 28
Mitchell, David, x
modernization, 36
monoethnic Japanese nation, 13
music references, 9

N

narrative strategies, 31
Narrative technique, 42
national identification, ix
national perception, ix
national specificity, 79
national stereotypes, 1
nihonjinron, 26
novel-grotesque, 32
Number9Dream, 4, 5, 6, 9, 10, 11, 14, 15, 16, 17, 21, 30, 31, 32, 33,

Index 91

35, 37, 40, 45, 51, 52, 56, 60, 62, 64, 68, 72, 73, 74, 78, 85, 88

O

on the side of the egg, 46
oriental cultures, ix
Orientalism, x, xiv, 5, 7, 23, 24, 25, 27, 78, 84, 87, 88
orientalization, 23
otherness, 24

P

parallel narratives, 67
paranoid horror, 39
planet Japan, 32
political critique, 64
polymedia, 30
postmodern discourse, 78
postmodern literary theories, 62
postmodern reconstruction, xiii
postmodern tradition, xv
pre-existing stereotypes, 27

R

realistic, xv
religious violence, 45
relocation, 29
remediation, xiv, 28, 29, 30, 31, 36
renewing the image of Japan, xiii
Representations, i, x, xiv, 40, 43, 53, 61, 62
Representations of Violence, xiv
representing Japan, xii
responsibility, 57
Ruth Benedict's *The Chrysanthemum and the Sword*, xi

S

Said, Edward, xii, 23
samurai, xiv
samurai ethics, 45
Sarin attack, 45
sci-fi literature, 26
self-orientalism, 25, 26
self-orientalization, 23, 24, 26
Self-Other" dichotomy, 20
semantics, 42
shifting signifiers, 30
signals of violence, 44
spirit of the Yamato warrior, 45
Stereotypes, 78
stereotypical meanings, xiv
"symbolic" violence, 44

T

Tatsumi, Takayuki, xi
Techno-Images, xiv
technological features, 36
Techno-Orientalism, xiv, 23, 26, 29
tehno-fantasy, 33
terrorism, xiii
the "distortion" of Japan, 51
the dichotomy of East-West perceptions, 79
the image of Japan, ix, 29, 30, 36, 42
the mirror of us, 55
the Other, 24
the real Japan, xv
the role of chance, 51
the wall and the egg, 46
2 Dystopian Features, 37

U

urban landscape, 42

V

violence, 43

W

war memory, 63
wartime aggression, 66
wartime atrocities, 60
Western discourse on Japan, 2
Westernization, ix
World War II, 45

Y

Yakuza, 75
Yasunari, Kawabata, 1

Z

Zizek, Slavoj, 43

www.ingramcontent.com/pod-product-compliance
Lightning Source LLC
Chambersburg PA
CBHW070303230426
43664CB00014B/2625